INSIGHTS INTO
Sensory
Issues
FOR PROFESSIONALS

INSIGHTS INTO
Sensory
Issues
FOR PROFESSIONALS

OUTSTANDING ARTICLES FROM THE PAGES OF
S.I. Focus MAGAZINE

Kathleen Morris, MS, CCC-SLP
Founder/Publisher, *S.I. Focus* Magazine

All marketing and publishing rights
guaranteed to and reserved by:

Sensory World
www.sensoryworld.com

721 W. Abram Street
Arlington, TX 76013
Toll-free: 800-489-0727
Phone: 817-277-0727
Fax: 817-277-2270
Web site: www.FHautism.com
E-mail: info@FHautism.com

Printed in the United States of America

Cover design: John Yacio
Interior design: Publication Services, Inc.

ISBN 13: 978-1-935567-19-6

CONTENTS

Part Two: General Insights

INTRODUCTION

What a privilege it is to have been asked by *Sensory World* to compile some of the best contributions that have been published by *S.I. Focus* magazine, thus far. Still in our early years, *S.I. Focus* has had the extreme pleasure of meeting and working with some of the finest professionals in the sensory community. Within these pages you will read selected articles from well-known occupational therapists, speech pathologists, physical therapists, researchers, scientists, and others. These contributing authors share a common bond with those of us who have worked to bring a quality quarterly magazine to our readers. Since I created the magazine in 2004, the mission has been to "enlighten, encourage, and empower" our readers. It is our authors who enable us to fulfill that mission.

As a pediatric therapist, clinic owner, and publisher, I have not achieved the realization of publishing the magazine on my own. From the very beginning, I have enjoyed the wisdom and skills of an outstanding editing team at my side. Although I select the articles that reach our readers, submissions have been carefully edited for content and form. Two amazing occupational therapists, Elaine Struthers, PhD (researcher and clinic owner), and Lawrene Kovalenko, OTR (graduate of the University of Southern California and student of Jean Ayres, PhD, OTR), have served as our technical editors for 5 years. You can trust that the content has been edited carefully for accuracy. I am also fortunate to have as our editor-in-chief Carol Kranowitz, MA, who wrote the book, *The Out-of-Sync Child*. Ms Kranowitz worked as a preschool teacher for 25 years, which exposed her to neurologically atypical children and inspired her to write a book regarding the idiosyncrasies of such children. She holds a master's degree in education and human development and is a prolific writer and editor. Her gift of writing enables our authors' contributions to flow and come alive for our readers.

Whether you are an *S.I. Focus* magazine enthusiast or you have never had the opportunity to read our publication, you will enjoy having this compilation of articles written specifically *by* and *for* professionals. In one convenient volume, you have insights from a variety of accomplished individuals, spanning a wide range of experience. I am hopeful that these insights will increase or substantiate your understanding of sensory issues in a variety of settings. One of my goals has been to incorporate perspectives from clinical, school, and home environments for our readers. It is the collaboration of professionals working in various environments that will truly change the world for individuals who face the challenges of misinterpreted information from their senses.

I am extremely pleased that you will have this book on your shelf at home or in a facility as a resource of information for understanding and working with individuals within the sensory community.

With warm regards,

Kathleen Morris
Publisher, *S.I. Focus*

PART ONE
Research and Clinical Insights

Speech Therapy and Occupational Therapy: What's the Connection? Oral-Motor, Sensory, and Feeding Skills

Robyn Merkel-Walsh, MA, CCC-SLP;
Sara Rosenfeld-Johnson, MS, CCC-SLP

What is the connection between speech-language pathologists (SLPs) and occupational therapists (OTs)? For sure, SLPs and OTs have a great deal in common. Both specialists search for the etiology of a problem, identify existing skill levels, and use that information to plan a client-centered program of therapeutic intervention. Both professionals are committed to helping their clients develop their maximum potential for basic human functions, such as eating, walking, and communicating. Quite often, these therapists co-treat clients, call each other for advice, and attend each other's conferences.

Additionally, these highly trained professionals target daily functions and are trained in the whole body system. Both understand anatomy and physiology, with special attention to the neurological makeup of the human being. Both look at automatic and volitional functions in assessing a client, and relate those to how this person can function daily in society.

For the OT, the concern deals with activities of daily living, and the fine motor system. For the SLP, special attention is paid to the functions of speech communication involving the muscles and nerves "from the neck up." The crucial connection for the SLP is that the mouth, a fine motor area, depends on what happens both from the neck up and from the neck down. The OT relies on the SLP for information on the client's cognitive ability and communicative capacity to attend to daily life activities.

One of the most important connections is the sensory system, which provides information on how an individual processes what he or she experiences. Many children and adults with autism and other neurological deficits suffer from sensory integration problems involving light, sound, touch, movement, taste, and/or smell. If the client cannot regulate him- or herself to the environment, it will be very difficult for that individual to communicate within that environment.

OTs are the experts in dealing with sensory disorders. They help children reduce hypersensitivity to stimuli or, if needed, alert children who are hyposensitive. Their techniques are also implemented by SLPs in terms of oral stimuli, including myofascial release techniques, feeding programs to increase diet preferences, and intraoral desensitizing for a child to tolerate oral-motor therapy tools. For example, both OTs and SLPs would use vibration to improve muscle awareness and prepare the client for touch cues provided within a therapy session. In a therapy session, an OT may use a blowing tool to gain midline orientation, abdominal grading, and visual tracking, while the SLP works on these skills in addition to using the same tools to improve jaw grading, lip rounding, tongue retraction, and jaw-lip-tongue dissociation.

SLPs and OTs share another common interest: feeding. Children with diagnosed feeding disorders are commonly seen for services by one or both of these professions through their state-sponsored Birth-to-Three Program. While both professions may have feeding skill development as their general goal, their short-term goals may vary slightly. The OT is primarily interested in maximizing hand-to-mouth control;

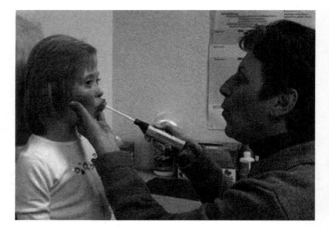

choosing the right feeding tools (eg, spoon, cup, fork); choosing the most appropriate food textures, tastes, and temperature; minimizing spillage; and improving feeding safety, with the ultimate goal of independence. An oral-motor–trained SLP acknowledges these goals, in addition to others that maximize how the food is controlled within the oral cavity. It is the basic premise of these therapists that the muscles that are used in feeding are the same muscles that are used in speech. For this reason, the SLP adds a sequence of oral exercises to improve jaw strength, lip closure, tongue retraction, and tongue-tip lateralization. As these skills are mastered, feeding safety improves.

At the Sara R. Johnson Oral-Motor and Speech-Language Associates, located in Tucson, Ariz, OTs and SLPs co-treat clients on a daily basis and cross-refer to facilitate progress with clients of all ages and ability levels. For a child, the therapists may make use of sensory integration activities such as vestibular activities and brushing techniques to prepare the sensory system for oral-motor activities. In adults, the goal may be for the OT to facilitate hand-to-mouth sequencing for feeding, while the SLP works on oral movements for bolus management.

The OT and SLP are closely interconnected, both in assessment and in treatment of clients. For an oral-motor specialist, assessing feeding or speech-skill levels without addressing the position of the body and the sensory system would be impossible. With increased knowledge comes increased success, so as these two professions continue to share information concerning their common interests, we will begin to see improved treatment models for all of our clients.

Robyn Merkel-Walsh, MA, CCC-SLP, is a speech pathologist and oral-motor specialist in New Jersey. She is employed by the Ridgefield Schools and has a private practice in Bergen County, NJ. She serves as a speaker for Innovative Therapists International and is the creator of The SMILE Program and Sensory Stix. She is currently working on the OPT Goals for Speech Therapy Program, available at www.talktools.net. Robyn has more than 10 years of experience and provides oral-motor and PROMPT services to the apraxic and autistic populations. She can be contacted at robynslp95@aol.com.

Sara Rosenfeld-Johnson practices at the SRJ Therapies Travel Clinic. She offers on-location visits when five families want an assessment or program-plan update. Sara is the author of Oral Placement Theory (OPT) for Speech Clarity and Feeding, Assessment and Treatment of the Jaw: Sensory Feeding and Speech, and Oral Placement Theory (OPT) for /s/ and /z/. This information may be found at www.TalkTools.net.

DSI in a Learning Disorders Clinic

Brock Eide, MD, MA;
Fernette Eide, MD

In her groundbreaking work, *Sensory Integration and the Child,* A. Jean Ayres estimated that 5%-10% of all children had disordered sensory integration (DSI). Carol Kranowitz, in her more recent DSI classic, *The-Out-of-Sync Child,* says estimates range between 12% and 30%, depending on the criteria used.

Although a precise tally of the number of children affected by DSI is difficult to come by for a variety of reasons, our own experience as physicians specializing in treating children with learning disorders leads us to agree with these authors that DSI is a vast—and vastly underrecognized—problem among preschool- and school-aged children. In this article, we describe our experience with DSI in children referred to our clinic by schools, physicians, or parents for evaluation of learning problems.

DSI Is *Common* in Kids with Learning Disorders

By using a set of diagnostic criteria that combined patient history and clinical observation, we determined that of our last 50 consecutive patients, 52% had difficulties with sensory integration severe enough to contribute to their learning problems. The frequency of DSI varied markedly according to age. In our 30 children under age 10, 70% had DSI, while in the remaining 20 children who were 10 years of age and older, only 20% had DSI.

The reasons for this striking difference are not entirely clear. It is possible that the prevalence of DSI diminishes with age because the sensory processing disorder tends to lessen or resolve. However, it is also possible that the sensory processing disorder persists, but, over time, many children tend to develop compensatory strategies for dealing with it, so that it no longer produces as many bothersome complications. Most experts in DSI lean toward the latter explanation. They believe that even in persons who have been treated with sensory integration therapy, some signs of the disorder are usually detectable, and that in untreated persons, these signs are usually readily apparent.

Our thoughts are somewhere in the middle. In our experience, the persistence of DSI tends to vary according to its severity. Severely affected children (who are, probably not coincidentally, the ones most likely to have come to the attention of the occupational therapists who have done most of the research in this field) are likely to have the most persistent and troublesome symptoms later in life. On the other hand, children with mild to moderate symptoms may improve symptomatically, even without therapy, to show few or no signs of DSI as adolescents of adults. Even among more mildly affected children, though, therapy may be helpful in speeding progress and preventing persistent, lifelong emotional and behavioral complications.

Diagnosing DSI in the Clinic: History

Of the various historical and physical data we use to diagnose DSI, no one type is able, by itself, to either "make or break" the diagnosis. We tend to view the information as a whole, to see whether a pattern of sensory dysfunction and behavioral difficulties consistent with the diagnosis of DSI emerges.

Currently, we gather historical information on the children we treat by having their parents answer a battery of 28 questions that probe sensory seeking or avoidance, balance and motor issues, and energy level. Table 1 displays some of the most revealing data from the 50 children in our sample.

In our current sample, parents of children diagnosed with DSI were over five times more likely than parents of children without DSI to say that their child had a weak grasp and floppy muscle tone, was insecure with slides and escalators, avoided rough play and playground equipment, or had unexpected falls while sitting in a chair or playing.

This historical information is interesting in several respects. First, the importance of balance and gravitational security issues in children with DSI suggests why vestibular and/or proprioceptive therapy, as pioneered by A. Jean Ayres, has been so successful in treating children with this disorder.

Table 1. Questionnaire Items Affirmed by Parents

Questionnaire Item	Children with DSI	Children without DSI
Unexpected falls out of chair or on playground	19%	0%
Floppy or loose muscle tone	29%	5%
Weak grasp	29%	5%
Doesn't like rough-housing	19%	5%
Doesn't like messy play or splashing in water	29%	10%
Fatigues easily	52%	19%
Avoids physical closeness	19%	10%
Covers ears to loud noises	52%	29%
Has tantrums	71%	46%

Second, it is important to note how many children with DSI have difficulties in the areas of motor energy and motor weakness. Our observations along these lines have led us to place a higher priority on motor conditioning and strengthening than that accorded by some traditional therapies.

Third, this information is important because of what it suggests about the etiology of DSI. Our own suspicion is that many of these clinical manifestations of DSI may occur as a result of a functional disorder of a specialized type of sensory nerve cell called a "spindle afferent." Spindle afferents are important in regulating muscle tone, in muscle fatigue, and in spatial localization at the joints—all functions that are affected in DSI. (We hope to return to address what is known or suspected about the causes of DSI in a subsequent issue of *S.I. Focus*.)

Returning to the data, all of our questions about tactile sensitivities and most of our questions about auditory sensitivities tended to yield affirmative responses by more parents of kids with DSI than those without. These questions, however, are not as specific for the disorder as the items mentioned previously.

Most of the questions we've tested regarding sensitivity for vision, smells, tastes, and sensory-seeking behavior have not been either sensitive or specific in identifying children with DSI.

Interestingly, most of the questions we ask parents regarding mood, affect (immediate expressions of emotion), and social and emotional behaviors tend to do a poor job of sorting out kids with DSI. Only one item is consistently affirmed by more parents of kids with DSI than those without: "Has tantrums." In our current sample, 71% of parents whose child has DSI said "yes" to this item. Only 46% of parents of children without DSI affirmed it.

Diagnosing DSI in the Clinic: Physical Exam

On physical examination (see Table 2), kids with DSI had poor or abnormal muscle tone almost twice as often as kids without DSI. Almost 60% of our sample had unusually floppy or spastic muscle tone. Nearly 40% had a condition called "scapular winging," in which the muscles of the back are too weak to hold the shoulder blades in place—roughly twice the frequency as that in children without DSI.

The proprioceptive or "spatial-positioning" problems in children with DSI were reflected in their almost universal inability to feel the positions of their fingers in space. This condition, called "finger agnosia," affects just over half of our population without DSI, reflecting the numbers of children we see with primary motor, graphomotor, and sensory problems. Still, it is almost twice

Table 2. Clinical Exam Findings

Clinical Finding	Children with DSI	Children without DSI
Abnormal muscle tone	58%	29%
Scapular winging	38%	21%
Finger agnosia	86%	52%
Hyperactivity	50%	9%
Impulsivity	31%	8%

as common in our patients with DSI. To understand what this condition means to a child, try to imagine what it must be like to attempt to write your name, draw a picture, button your shirt, or tie your shoes with fingers that don't know where they are in space or in what directions they're moving.

Although our parent questionnaires didn't demonstrate a clear difference in sensory-seeking behaviors between kids with DSI and those without, our physical examination *did* show evidence of sensory-seeking behavior in a full 85% of children with DSI. Only 54% of children without DSI showed such behavior. These activities included chair-spinning, table- and paper-picking, fidgeting, kicking (table, chair, and examiner), crashing, and bumping.

Finally, although results of our historical questionnaire did not show variations in impulsive or hyperactive behaviors that correlated with the DSI diagnosis, our examinations yielded marked discrepancies in such behaviors. Impulsive behaviors, such as grabbing items without asking, beginning test segments without waiting, and answering questions in an unplanned manner, were almost four times more common in children with DSI. Hyperactive behaviors, such as running around the exam room, jumping and crashing into things, and fidgeting, were over five times more common in kids with DSI.

Attentional difficulties, which were present in essentially all children in our study, did not differ superficially between groups. These findings raise important issues regarding the relationship of DSI and attention-deficit/hyperactivity disorder (ADHD), as the three cardinal manifestations of ADHD are impulsivity, hyperactivity, and attentional disorder. Because this is such an important issue for parents, therapists, and educators, we are going to wait to address this topic until we can give it the detailed consideration it deserves in the next issue of *S.I. Focus*.

Conclusion

DSI is remarkably common in the children we see with learning problems, especially in children under the age of 10. The obvious, indeed inescapable, conclusion is that DSI contributes significantly to the learning problems facing many of our children. We are encouraged by signs that this long-neglected and profoundly important condition is finally beginning to receive the attention it deserves. We are optimistic that the future will bring many more advances in our understanding of this disorder and in our ability to help the children it affects.

Brock Eide, MD, MA, is a graduate of the University of Washington and the University of Washington School of Medicine. He trained at the University of Pennsylvania and the University of California, San Francisco. He was a MacLean Fellow and received his master's degree from the University of Chicago.

Fernette Eide, MD, is a graduate of Harvard-Radcliffe College and the University of California, San Francisco (UCSF), Medical School. She trained in neurology at both the University of Pennsylvania and UCSF. She is currently a clinical assistant professor in neurology at the University of Washington.

The Drs Eide share a private practice, The Eide Neurolearning Clinic, specializing in children's cognition and learning in Edmonds, Wash, and have created a Web site at www.neurolearning. com and a blog at EideNeurolearning.blogspot.com. They have also authored a book, The Mislabeled Child. To contact the Eides by e-mail, write to drseide@gmail.com.

A Review of Research on Sensory Modulation Disorders in Adults

Moya Kinnealey, PhD, OTR/L; Sinclair Smith, ScD

With our colleagues over the past years, we have conducted research and published articles on sensory modulation disorders (SMDs) in adults. We focused on sensory defensiveness (SD), or overresponsivity, as this modulation disorder was described most frequently in the literature and had symptoms most clearly identifiable by clinicians. These symptoms include a strong emotional reaction to nonnoxious environmental stimuli, such as noise—not only loud noises, but the sound of someone chewing, the crinkling of a candy wrapper, or the buzz inside a stoplight; touch, such as hair care and tags and seams in clothing; smells, tastes, and textures that most people do not notice; movement, such as the feeling of being in elevators and on escalators and uneven surfaces; and visual stimuli, such as contrasts, reflections, and bright lights.

Initially, our interest was sparked by parental reports of children with sensory defensiveness who displayed social-emotional issues that interfered with their acceptance and progress in school. The medical advice parents received was that their child would grow out of "it." It became apparent that untreated children did not grow out of it. Instead, the sensory issues and the social/emotional correlates developed at different stages of their lives into symptoms that fit a variety of diagnostic categories.

For example, children with regulatory disorders (a diagnosis for 0-3–year-olds) might later be labeled as having Oppositional Defiant Disorder (ODD) or attention-deficit/hyperactivity disorder (ADHD). In adolescence, anxiety, depression, and social issues might trigger a diagnosis. By adulthood, they may manifest other mental health diagnoses. Because SMD and sensory processing or sensory integration disorders[1] are not medical or psychological diagnoses, the diagnoses assigned to these adults are based on symptoms that most often (but not always) include the symptoms of SD.

We were compelled to explore and understand the effects of SD in adulthood. We had to provide evidence that this phenomenon existed independently of other related phenomena, such as abuse or psychological and/or psychiatric disorders. We also had to determine a reliable and objective way of identifying SD. We developed an assessment, the ADULT-SI (Adult Defensiveness: Understanding Learning and Treating—Sensory Interview) and a screening questionnaire, the Adult Sensory Questionnaire (ASQ). We established their reliability and validity through a series of studies, including validation with physiological measures.[2]

The score-able interview format of the ADULT-SI provides valuable insight through descriptions by the adult with SD of his or her subjective responses to sensory stimuli in the context of daily life. For example, the examiner asks, "Do you enjoy pets? What do you like or dislike about them? How does the pet make you feel?" The evaluator listens for responses related to touch, smell, behavior, physical interaction, predictability, etc, that the evaluators judge as defensive. Unlike other test formats, the ADULT-SI captures this complexity and interplay of atypical sensory responses.

We next started to describe and identify the qualitative and quantitative differences between adults with SD and those without. This endeavor gave us insight into how profoundly different life experiences were for defensive people. The way they described their perception of everyday experiences was different—irritating, distracting, and disorganizing. They spent an inordinate amount of time coping with these responses, which left them exhausted and frequently isolated.[3] Adults with SD were concerned about their mental well being because they were aware from early in life that their perceptions of sensory experiences were different and peculiar by others' standards. Sensory defensiveness was found to be associated with anxiety, depression, and social-emotional issues.[4] It was found to interfere with occupational performance[5] and to affect health-related quality of life.[6]

In treating adults with SMD and, specifically, SD, we have found that adults need to understand the phenomenon and its effects on their lives to be in control and to choose to initiate intervention. Adults need to understand the neurobehavioral substrates of this condition, how they can advocate for themselves, and how they can organize their lives to reduce the negative effects of SD. They require intervention strategies that fit into their daily life routines and that can be drawn upon in times of need. They also need emotional support to begin treatment. At the same time, many people with SD are so exhausted by coping and so fearful of change that they become very controlling, nonspontaneous, and apprehensive of anything new. They cite that they are too busy, would prefer taking a pill, and are seeking help or counseling from someone who understands them. In these situations, changing or interfering with their routine is extremely difficult. There seems to be inertia, perhaps due to a belief that nothing they do can make life better and that the best they can hope for is that things don't get worse. Routines are predictable and safe; initiating new routines of activities becomes a stumbling block to intervention.

For people with SD who participate in occupational therapy intervention, we found that symptoms of sensory defensiveness and anxiety are reduced significantly, and some aspects of health-related quality of life improve. One case study also demonstrated significant changes in physiological responses to stimuli after treatment, suggesting that treatment can affect the physiological response that may underlie the behavioral response. A current study by Dr Sinclair Smith, the Director of the Neuro-muscular Laboratory in the Department of Occupational Therapy, Temple University, uses a variety of physiological measures to measure pre- and postintervention differences, including heart rate, blood flow, and electrodermal skin conductance of adults with and those without SD.

Postintervention descriptions by subjects after treatment are by far the most interesting and perhaps important. They report that the "edge" on life is gone. They describe participating readily and spontaneously in an event or activity that they would have avoided previously or that would have overwhelmed them. They describe increased energy levels and the ability to do more, and they are happier. Similar results were found in a study of the effects of treatment on children, reinforced by parental descriptions of behavioral changes in their children in the weeks after intervention.[7] We call this outcome "adaptability," which appears to allow for greater participation in activities and occupations.

Some adults with SD are "self-treaters." These individuals participate in regular strenuous physical activity, such as marathons, daily workouts at gymnasiums, rough contact sports, etc. Self-treaters do not display the social and emotional aspects of the phenomenon, even though the descriptions of their sensory perceptions and responses are typical of SD. The implication is that vigorous and purposeful activities can be an effective part of a sensory diet that lessens the debilitating effects of SD.

We are gradually understanding sensory modulation disorders and sensory defensiveness, yet several assumptions and realities continue to impede progress. First, SMD is not recognized as a diagnosis. Second, SMD symptoms are subsumed within a variety of diagnostic categories in the *Diagnostic and Statistical Manual of Mental Disorders,* 4th edition (or DSM-IV), and standard treatment does not address the sensory aspect. Third, it is assumed that by adulthood it is too late to treat sensory defensiveness. In fact, we have found excellent results in adults who participate in treatment. Finally, funding to research this phenomenon is insufficient, and, as a result, knowledge grows slowly. Because SD negatively affects so many lives even though it can be modified, it is important to continue educating both professionals and nonprofessionals about SD and to persevere in researching effective intervention strategies.

References

1. Miller LJ, McIntosh DN. The diagnosis, treatment, and etiology of sensory modulation disorder. *Sensory Integration Special Interest Section Q.* 1998:21:1–3.

2. Kinnealey M, Smith S. Sensory defensive and non-defensive adults: physiological and behavioral differences. Presented at: 13th World Congress of Occupational Therapists; June 23–38, 2002; Stockholm, Sweden.

3. Kinnealey M, Oliver B, Wilbarger P. A phenomenological study of sensory defensiveness in adults. *Am J Occup Ther.* 1995;49:444–551.

4. Kinnealey M, Fuiek M. The relationship between sensory defensiveness, anxiety, depression and the perception of pain in adults. *Occup Ther Int.* 1999;6:196–206.

5. Pfeiffer B. The impact of dysfunction in sensory integration on occupations in childhood through adulthood: a case study. American Occupational Therapy Association, Sensory Integration Special Interest Section Newsletter. 2001;25(1):1–2.

6. Pfeiffer B, Kinnealey M. Treatment of sensory defensiveness in adults. *Occup Ther Int.* 2003;10(3):175–184.

7. Kinnealey M, Koenig KP, Huecker GE. Changes in special needs children following intensive short-term intervention. *J Dev Learning Disord.* 1999;3(1):85–103.

Moya Kinnealey, PhD, OTR/L, is chair and associate professor in the Department of Occupational Therapy at Temple University, where she has administrative, teaching, and research responsibilities.

Sinclair Smith, ScD, is assistant professor and director of the Neuro-muscular Laboratory in the Department of Occupational Therapy at Temple University, where he has research and teaching responsibilities.

Hyperactivity, Impulsivity, and DSI

Brock Eide, MD, MA; Fernette Eide, MD

In the last issue of *S.I. Focus,* we described our experience of dysfunction of sensory integration (DSI) in a group of 50 consecutive children seen in our general learning disorders clinic.[1] We reported that 52% of these children (70% of those under 10) had problems with DSI severe enough to contribute to their learning difficulties. We also reported that children with DSI were far more likely than those without DSI to show evidence of hyperactivity or impulsivity on physical examination. During our exam, 50% of the children with DSI engaged in hyperactive behaviors, such as running around the exam room, jumping and crashing into things, and extreme fidgeting; while only 9% of the children without DSI showed such behaviors. We observed impulsive behaviors, such as grabbing items without asking, beginning test questions without waiting, and answering questions in an unplanned manner, in 31% of children with DSI but in only 8% of children without DSI.

In that article, we pointed out that these findings raise important questions regarding the relationship between DSI and attention-deficit/hyperactivity disorder (ADHD), the cardinal manifestations of ADHD being hyperactivity, impulsivity, and distractibility or attentional impairment. In this article, we would like to address these questions in further detail, drawing additional information from our review of 50 children. We would like to state at the start of this discussion that this informal review of 50 cases clearly does not constitute definitive proof of any particular hypotheses. However, we do feel that our experience is highly suggestive and has important implications for parents, teachers, and clinicians who care for children with DSI, regarding the need for careful screening and evaluation of these children. With this caution in mind, we would like to turn to the data.

In our group of 50 children, 18 showed evidence of hyperactivity (eight children), impulsivity (three children), or both (seven children) on physical examination. Perhaps the most remarkable thing about this group of children is the high prevalence—indeed the universality—of clinically significant sensory or neurologic impairments. Table 1 summarizes the categories of sensory and neurologic impairments found in these children.

Table 1. Neurologic Findings among 18 Children with Hyperactivity and/or Impulsivity

No. of Children	Neurologic Findings
15 (83%)	Dysfunctional Sensory Integration
6 (33%)	Attention-Deficit/Hyperactivity Disorder
12 (67%)	Visual Dysfunction
12 (67%)	Auditory Dysfunction
12 (67%)	Other Clinically Significant Neurological Impairments

Three of these children (17%) had previously been diagnosed with ADHD. Each of these three had been given stimulant medication for this disorder. On the basis of our assessment, three additional children from this group were strongly suspected of having ADHD and were referred back to their primary care providers for consideration of a trial of stimulant medications.

Fifteen of the 18 children (83%) were diagnosed with DSI. Importantly, this subgroup of 15 children included all seven who showed both impulsivity and hyperactivity on clinical examination, all three who had previously been diagnosed with ADHD, and all three who had not received a previous diagnosis but whom we suspected of having ADHD.

Twelve of the 18 children (67%) had clinically significant visual abnormalities. These abnormalities included problems with tracking, convergence, binocularity, astigmatism, and acuity. Most of these problems were unsuspected previously, and each of them was marked enough to impact learning performance.

Twelve of these 18 children (67%) also showed difficulties of auditory functioning consistent with a diagnosis of central auditory processing deficit (CAPD). During testing, these children repeatedly demonstrated behaviors characteristic of children with CAPD, including prolonged auditory latency, frequent mishearing, hyperacusis, auditory distractibility, impaired inference and comprehension when listening compared with reading, and marked discrepancy between auditory short-term memory (their ability to repeat back like a tape recorder) and auditory comprehension. In many of these children, the diagnosis of CAPD has subsequently been confirmed by means of audiometric testing. Two additional children were found to have combined disorders of expressive and receptive language, and, in addition to speech difficulties, they displayed many symptoms similar to those in children with CAPD.

Evidence of clinically significant neurological dysfunction (in addition to those related directly to DSI and ADHD) was also found in 12 of the 18 children (67%). Four had mild hemiparesis, and one had monoparesis. Two had evidence of clinically significant bihemispheric injuries. Two had combined receptive and expressive language difficulties. One was diagnosed with a seizure disorder, one had Tourette syndrome, one had a clinically significant sensory neuropathy, and one had fetal alcohol syndrome. Again, most of these abnormalities had been undiagnosed previously.

In total, all but one of the 18 children displayed marked visual or auditory sensory difficulties, and the excluded child showed deficits from fetal alcohol syndrome so diffuse that adequate sensory examination was difficult. Each of the children with DSI had either a visual or auditory sensory disorder, and seven of these 15 children had both.

These findings raise several important points regarding the evaluation and management of children with hyperactivity and impulsivity. The first and most important of these points is the absolute necessity of recognizing how frequently such children have sensory and neurological impairments other than primary attentional disorders. In our sample of 18 children, impairments of this kind were found in every child, and most had clinically significant impairments in several systems.

It is, of course, possible that the children in our sample are not entirely representative of children with hyperactivity and impulsivity in the general population. Eight of the 18 children (44%) have been placed in alternative learning environments as a result of their disabilities (see Table 2). Still, we have several reasons to suspect that they are representative enough to be revealing. First, many of the children in our study group were self-referred, and we were the first evaluators for some. While we do have a specialty clinic and we therefore see many patients by referral, we are a community-based practice rather than an academic one, and as such, we are a first line of referral for children with difficulties. Second, 10 of the children (56%) in our sample are enrolled in regular classes in public elementary or large private schools, and as such, are probably a reasonable sample of children in typical educational settings. Third, others have previously noted high frequencies of neurologic impairments in children diagnosed with ADHD.[2] In one particularly revealing article, an ophthalmologist from the University of California at San Diego documented visual-tracking abnormalities in nearly half of a sample of randomly selected children with ADHD.[3]

Our findings also suggest several important points about DSI. First, they highlight the fact that DSI is frequently seen as a secondary manifestation of neurologic impairment, and they stress the importance of looking for evidence of specific sensory impairments in children with DSI. When brain development is impaired, either through injury or through the failure of primary sensory systems to promote appropriate growth of central processing centers, the brain attempts to compensate for this impairment by remodeling or rewiring.[4-7] Compensatory rewiring can result in improved function in some respects, but it can also result in function that is poorly regulated if the new connections lack the appropriate balance of stimulatory and inhibitory influences. When imbalance occurs in areas that regulate sensory or sensorimotor functions, DSI results, with its classic manifestations of hyper- and hyposensitivities and their resulting sensory-avoidant and sensory-seeking behaviors.[8] In children with DSI, behaviors often labeled hyperactive appear to be unreflective attempts to maintain sufficient arousal of their understimulated alertness centers to allow their brains to function in a useful way. That's why, in our experience,

Table 2. School Placement of 18 Children with Hyperactivity and/or Impulsivity

No. of Children	School Placement
10 (56%)	Public or Large Private School
4 (22%)	Special Developmental School
3 (17%)	Home School
1 (5%)	Small Private School

"hyperactive" behaviors in children with DSI frequently sharpen their attention and improve focus upon testing, rather than impair their attention and performance.

This process of impairment and rewiring also helps explain the frequent presence of distractibility in children with DSI and/or sensory impairments. A clear example of the way such rewiring results in secondary distractibility is seen in persons who are deaf. When a child is born deaf, cerebral cortical areas usually reserved for auditory processing are recruited for other functions, such as vision.[9-10] Visual sensitivity may be somewhat improved in the central visual fields, but only at the expense of heightened visual distractibility at the periphery. This is why hearing-impaired readers often become paralyzed when trying to read visually busy books and worksheets. This pattern of one sensory system compensating for the deficiencies of another can also be observed among the blind.[11]

The high rates of impulsivity, hyperactivity, and distractibility seen in children with DSI can often make it difficult to determine in particular children whether these behaviors are simply manifestations of DSI or whether they are signs of a primary attentional disorder like ADHD. In our experience, the purely behavioral criteria for ADHD listed in the *Diagnostic and Statistical Manual of Mental Disorders*, 4th edition (or DSM-IV), are not particularly useful in making these distinctions. Nearly all of the children in our sample with hyperactivity and/or impulsivity would meet these criteria, yet we do not believe that most of these children show sufficient evidence of a primary attentional disorder to merit a diagnosis of ADHD. Although there are as yet no generally accepted criteria for distinguishing between these conditions, and although in our sample 33% of children were diagnosed with both, we have found two criteria useful in distinguishing children whose hyperactivity appears to be caused by DSI from those in whom it appears to result from primary attentional disorders. First, we believe the diagnosis of ADHD is best suited for children who show generalized attentional impairment in all areas of testing, rather than those who have selective attentional problems only, with tasks that stress struggling visual or auditory systems. Second, we find the ADHD diagnosis better suited for those children whose self-stimulatory and hyperactive behaviors produce a worsening of performance instead of an improvement.

Just the other day, we had a young patient who exceeded age norms on many portions of our tests while working nonstop on the most elaborate piece of Theraputty pizza (complete with pepperoni and mushrooms) ever made. Hyperactive? Yes. Sensory seeking? Yes. Attentional impairment? Not that we can detect.

What's the bottom line? In children with impulsivity and hyperactivity, the answer should never simply be a straight line to stimulants. It is crucial to evaluate such children for disorders of sensory integration and other visual, auditory, or somatosensory impairments.

References

1. Eide B, Eide F. DSI in a learning disorders clinic. *S.I. Focus.* 2004;1(2):9–11.

2. Voeller K. Attention deficit. *Continuum.* 2002;8(5):74–112.

3. Granet DB. Convergence insufficiency and ADHD. In: Proceedings from the American Academy of Pediatric Ophthalmology and Strabismus; April 12–16, 2000; St Louis, MO. Abstract.

4. Ragazzoni A, et al. Congenital hemiparesis: different functional reorganization of somatosensory and motor pathways. *Clin Neurophysiol.* 2002;113(8):1273–1278.

5. Briellmann R, et al. Brain reorganisation in cerebral palsy: a high-field functional MRI study. *Neuropediatr.* 2002;33(3):162–165.

6. Grodd S, et al. Two types of ipsilateral reorganization in congenital hemiparesis: a TM/S and fMRI Study. *Brain.* 2002;125(10):2222–2237.

7. Rockstroh B. Reorganization of human cerebral cortex: the range of changes following use and injury. *Neuroscientist.* 2004;10(2):129–141.

8. Eide FF. Sensory integration: current concepts and practical implications. *Sensory Integration Special Interest Section Q.* 2003;16(3):1–3.

9. Shibata DK, et al. Functional MR imaging of vision in the deaf. *Acad Radiol.* 2001;8(7): 598–604.

10. Finney EM, et al. Visual stimuli activate auditory cortex in the deaf. *Nat Neurosci.* 2001;4(12):1171–1173.

11. Ross DA, et al. Cortical plasticity in an early blind musician: an fMRI study. *Magn Reson Imaging.* 2003;11(7):821–828.

The Drs Eide share a private practice, The Eide Neurolearning Clinic, specializing in children's cognition and learning in Edmonds, Wash, and created the Web site www.neurolearning.com and a blog at EideNeurolearning.blogspot.com. They have also authored a book, The Mislabeled Child. To contact the Eides by e-mail, write to drseide@gmail.com.

Using Sensory Integration Theory to Help Kate See

Elaine Jean Struthers, PhD, OTR/L

Our sense of who we are in the world is largely influenced by our physical body, which carries us through our journey in life. The sensory nature of our body is not static but an individually unique life process. Although we often talk of the various sensory systems as if they were discrete, or separate, all sensory data are intermingled at several different levels of the nervous system, and difficulties in one sensory area usually translate into multiple functional problems. An example is 5-year-old Kate, recently encountered in our clinic, who had visual challenges that affected her behavior and success in many areas of function.

The visual system is tied to many systems, including the vestibular (balance and movement senses) and auditory (hearing) processing pathways at the level of nuclei, or neural relay stations, in the brain stem. Sight and sound are critical components of our sense of self. Movement, or the vestibular sense, coordinates sight and sound to the outer and inner worlds of self in a way that promotes survival and mediates our experience and relationships with people, places, and things.[1] When any condition outside the "norm" occurs in the visual system, our ability to interact with the external world is altered or impaired in many ways.[2-3]

Common visual defects can have profound developmental and behavioral effects.

The term "amblyopic" describes a developmental disorder of spatial vision in which reduced visual function exists without observable pathology and despite full optical correction. The condition is thought to affect around 1%-3% of the population and is almost always associated with the presence of strabismus (misalignment of the visual axes) and/ or anisometropia (significant difference in refractive error between the eyes). Although much has been learned about the visual characteristics of amblyopes, many questions remain, particularly with regard to the precise nature of the underlying neural changes that can explain the behavioral deficit.[4]

Research into the nature of individual perceptual experience indicates that "perception in human amblyopia may have its origin in errors in the neural coding of orientation in the visual cortex.[5] These errors are related to interpretation of vertical and horizontal perception. A test, termed "grating," was used to evaluate the orientation of lines in visual perception in one research study. A perceptual error rate of about 70% was found in persons with amblyopia when compared with persons with typical vision (Ibid). There appears to be wide individual variation in error type, but errors may incline vertical linear visual elements into angular distortions and also impact binocularity.

Understanding the close relationship between hearing, movement, and vision through the vestibular nuclei makes it easy to imagine how confusing unreliable vision might be when we are evaluating the functional behavior of a child. When what he sees is inconsistent with sound and movement information, his nervous system can't easily calculate or adapt to the related forces of gravity and velocity to help him relate to his surroundings. As he is trying to sort the conflicting sensory information, the child may become preoccupied. The result may be behaviors that appear to friends, family, or teachers as "spaced-out," clumsy, or even hysterical if the child's confusion triggers a state of fear and if the behavior becomes guided primarily by the autonomic nervous system, as demonstrated by fight or flight responses.[6] As the child goes into a reactive state we see autonomic nervous system (ANS) symptoms, which are the physiological symptoms that all good therapists watch for, such as respiration changes, pupillary dilation, and asymmetrical flushing. These symptoms tell us a child is in "overload."

ANS refers to the more automatic and phylogenetically older portions of the nervous system (brain stem–centered responses, etc), and we commonly refer to them as the fight, flight, and fright responses, including fear, hysteria, and rage. These responses are like an automatic copilot or default when higher-level cortical processes fail to mediate the environmental demands.

Kate was referred to our clinic for sensory integration–based therapy after a psychologist and psychiatrist evaluated, diagnosed, and treated her for high-functioning autism. She was intelligent and had good reading, writing, and comprehension skills. She had many abilities in fine and gross motor activities, including beading, running, and doing puzzles. However, when we presented Kate with challenges that took her out of close visual proximity with her own body and asked her to perform gross motor tasks, such as climbing a ladder or riding a bicycle, we had some surprising results.

As Kate reached the fourth rung on the ladder and looked back down at us, she began to scream and cry for her mother. When she rode a bicycle with training wheels, she complained of feeling dizzy. As she approached within 5 feet of the enclosed cycle area wall, she screamed and appeared to have a reflexive response that threw her off-balance so badly she fell over. Much crying, screaming, and reference to mother accompanied all of these events. We decided to determine if the underlying sensory substrate that was fueling Kate's fear was in her sense of movement and balance or in her visual system alone.

We asked her to climb a ladder without looking down, and to enter a tunnel that was made of a stretchy, flowered fabric. Kate climbed up skillfully, opened the tunnel, peered in, and began to scream immediately. She could not be consoled until one of us opened the other end of the tunnel and looked in so she could see our face. She said she thought the tunnel went on "forever." Reluctantly, she crawled through the tunnel. As long as she had a point of reference (a face at the end of the tunnel), she felt secure. When we removed the point of reference again, she became frantic and said she didn't know which way to go and that she couldn't breathe.

Because we knew that vision and movement are tied together, we understood that Kate was trying to rely on her vision to register movement. She could climb skillfully and confidently when she did not look down and kept her vision proximally focused on the ladder rungs. But when she switched from primarily gravity and touch sensations to primarily vision sensations to relay position-in-space information, we discovered that Kate became so disoriented and scared that she was quite literally unsafe. Through several activities we engaged her in, we found that heights, angles, and visual distortions (such as the multipatterned, closed fabric tunnels) caused pronounced panic and dyspraxia (clumsiness).

When she had a distal point of focus (a friendly face), and when the tunnel eliminated extra visual clutter, she could easily negotiate the unpredictable movement and gravity sensations. With increasing visual distance and complexity, however, Kate's performance, mastery, and confidence quickly began to disintegrate.

As clinicians, this information helped us greatly in designing treatment for Kate. We could better understand what her perceptual world was like, why she would scream and panic when she looked up the hilly road by their home and saw a car speeding down it around a curve. It is likely that the angle and grade of the landscape were exaggerated or distorted as a result of Kate's amblyopia. Linear elements in the landscape would be seen in ways inconsistent with information that Kate's nervous system received kinesthetically or from hearing.

To get a clearer picture of the underlying systems and to facilitate a complete treatment approach, we collaborated with other professionals and institutions. We referred Kate for additional evaluations. We requested that she undergo a full Sensory Integration and Praxis Test (SIPT)[7] administered by a skilled administrator, a standardized visual perception test in the school setting, and vision testing by a behavioral ophthalmologist. Kate received below-average scores on the space visualization and postrotary nystagmus (a test of vestibular-ocular function) portions of the SIPT. The public school declined to provide a standard visual perceptual test, but several months later the school nurse determined that Kate was not able to adequately read the Snellen, or "Big E," eye chart. At that point she was sent for complete vision testing. Kate was examined by both an ophthalmologist and a behavioral vision therapist and was diagnosed with left amblyopia.

As clinicians, we defined our role as being able to identify Kate's areas of sensorimotor challenge and to collaborate with institutions and practitioners to define the dysfunctional sensorimotor substrates of the nervous system. Then we designed treatment strategies that would strengthen function and integration of challenged sensorimotor systems. In Kate's case, we engaged her in activities that enhanced vestibular-ocular function. We supported therapies designed by the behavioral optometrist, including glasses, intermittent patching of one eye, and visual motor games. We worked on developing Kate's confidence through guided engagement with movement and visual play, which allowed successful mastery of new skills. Finally, and very importantly, we increased the neurological value of these activities by making sure to have a lot of fun.

References

1. Ayres AJ. *Sensory Integration and Learning Disorders*. Los Angeles, CA: WPS Publishing; 1972.

2. Hubel DH, Wiesel TN. Binocular interaction in striate cortex of kittens reared with artificial squint. *J Neurophysiol*. 1965;28:1041–1059.

3. Levi DM, Klein SA, Yap YL. Positional uncertainty in peripheral and amblyopic vision. *Vis Res*. 1987;27:581–597.

4. Barret BT, Pacey IE, Bradley A, Thibos LN, Morrill P. Nonveridical perception in human amblyopia. *Invest Opthalmol Vis Sci*. 2003;44:1555-1567.

5. Bradley A, Barret BT, Pacey IE, Thibos LN, Morrill P. Non-veridical perception in human amblyopia: perceptual evidence of neural changes in visual cortex. *J Vis*. 2003;3(9).

6. Schulkin J. *Rethinking Homeostasis*. Cambridge, MA: MIT Press; 2003.

7. Ayres AJ. Sensory Integration and Praxis Test. Los Angeles, CA: WPS Publishing; 1989.

Elaine Jean Struthers, PhD, OTR/L, has spent 2 decades using sensorimotor techniques with captive nonhuman primates and children with autism spectrum disorders. Currently, she maintains a private pediatric practice and works at the Esperenza Clinic for Sensory Integration Dysfunction & Other Developmental Delays. She is available for consultation and presentations and may be reached through www.islanddot.com.

Sensory Stories:
A New Tool to Improve Participation for Children with Overresponsive Sensory Modulation

Deborah Marr, ScD, OTR/L;
Victoria L. Nackley, MS, OTR/L

Several years ago we were conducting a workshop for state employees in a variety of human service positions. The topic addressed how sensory processing variations can affect the behavior of clients and fellow employees. These were not health professionals, so we began with a solid foundation of the sensory systems. Over the 2-day workshop, we described many sensory strategies a person or client could use to minimize the effects of overresponsive sensory modulation. At another point in the workshop, we also described an interesting intervention: social stories. Then the light bulb went off! Why couldn't we write a type of social story to teach people sensory strategies to use to overcome their overresponsive reactions? With that realization, Sensory Stories were born.

Over the next few years, Sensory Stories evolved into a very concrete program that is designed to meet the needs of children with overresponsive sensory modulation. In a nutshell, Sensory Stories are simple stories on a CD-ROM with a specified content format (for story titles, see Figures 1–3). When read to children in print format or on the computer, the Sensory Story teaches them key sensory strategies. When read to children on a regular basis, the children learn to self-implement the calming sensory strategies to help them tolerate an otherwise difficult-to-tolerate occupation. With a conservative estimate of 5% of the kindergarten population having a sensory processing issue,[1] there is a great need for such an approach.

Sensory Stories follow a specific format that takes children through an everyday activity in sequential fashion. Each story opens with a brief description of the everyday activity. This is followed by an identification of the sensory experiences children may have when engaging in that everyday activity. It is acknowledged in the story that these experiences may be unpleasant. Then several sensory strategies are suggested that should be done to get ready for the activity. As the activity is described further, more strategies are suggested. Once the activity is over, some final strategies are recommended. The story ends with a positive statement about the activity.

Occupational therapists frequently work with children with overresponsive sensory modulation disorders. Some of these children have other primary diagnoses, such as attention-deficit/

- Bathing
- Combing Hair
- Ear Cleaning
- Eating
- Getting Dressed in the Morning
- Showering
- Sleeping
- Tooth Brushing
- Washing Hair
- Nail Care

Figure 1. Sensory Story Titles Related to Home

- Assemblies
- Being in Lines
- Cafeteria
- Circle Time / Floor Time
- Desk Time
- Moving in the School
- Outdoor Recess
- School Bus Ride
- Physical Education Class
- Eating Time

Figure 2. Sensory Story Titles Related to School

- Getting a Haircut
- Going to a Restaurant
- Going to a Store
- Going to a Party
- Going to Places of Worship
- Going to the Dentist
- Going to the Doctor
- Riding in an Elevator
- Riding in a Car
- Riding on an Escalator

Figure 3. Sensory Story Titles Related to Community

hyperactivity disorder, autism, or Fragile X syndrome.[2] The multifaceted emotional and behavioral challenges of daily life can make it difficult to find the best combination of programs to meet the needs of all families. Many good programs are offered to make occupations more successful, including direct intervention, sensory diets, and the Wilbarger protocol. Sensory Stories are meant to be an additional item in a therapist's "bag of tricks."

Key Features of Sensory Stories

Each Sensory Story defines one activity that is a common problem in the home, school, or community. The design of Sensory Stories includes basic features that the authors believe will assist children in participating in daily-life activities. These features are:

Sensory Strategies. Sensory strategies are embedded within each Sensory Story to prepare children before, during, and after the activity. The strategies embody principles of sensory integration theory for children who need calming and/or inhibitory sensory input. Thus, Sensory strategies use deep-touch input, slow linear vestibular input, and heavy proprioceptive input in the form of active resistance to movement.

Self-Choice. Suggestions made throughout each Sensory Story allow children to make a choice. Phrases such as, "I can…" or "I like to…" suggest rather than direct children to use a strategy. Also, each CD-ROM includes a Strategy List of more than 70 strategies that children may select to add to their story. Success is more likely to happen when children sense their power in the process.

Self-Implementation. Children are solely in charge of doing each strategy within the Sensory Story. They decide when to implement the strategy, how intensely the sensory input is applied, and when to stop the strategy.

Customization. By virtue of being in CD-ROM format, stories can be customized for individual children. Customizing allows many possibilities: rewording of the text to match the education level and culture, selection of additional or alternate strategies for the story, and replacing line drawings with photographs. Children can participate in the customization process by making these changes on the computer or by decorating the Sensory Story once it is printed.

Socially Acceptable Strategies. The strategies are socially acceptable and draw as little attention as possible to enhance children's successful participation. When using the strategies, children can inconspicuously push up on their chair, wear a heavy fanny pack, or squeeze their legs together tightly, for example.

The Use of Line Drawings. Simple line drawings zero in on the specific detail of the strategy. The drawings provide culture- and gender-neutral models to demonstrate the story's content. Line drawings allow children to customize the story once it is printed by coloring in facial features, hair, and clothes.

The Innate Desire of Children. We believe that all children innately want to participate with peers and be successful in their environment at home, in school, and in the community. Once children try Sensory Stories and experience a positive outcome, they are more likely to continue to implement the strategies. The feelings of success have the potential to favorably influence other areas of their lives, changing children's outlook on participation in everyday activities.

Improving Awareness. In most cases, each Sensory Story depicts potentially negative sensory experiences associated with the activity to teach the reasons behind the experiences. With raised awareness, people can understand what the child may perceive as unpleasant about the activity, as well as when those same negative sensory experiences occur in other situations. Future negative reactions can be stopped ahead of time when people are more aware of the underlying causes.

Evidence on Effectiveness

An initial field-testing pilot study was conducted, where therapists across the country tried Sensory Stories and provided feedback. Of the 72 Sensory Story trials, 83% produced slight to significant positive change, as reported by the occupational therapists.[3] Some of the qualitative comments made by the therapists are presented in Figure 4. In another study, an applied behavioral analysis,

The child . . .	
• Complains less; is more tolerant	• No longer has tantrums at bedtime, sleeps better
• Stayed calmer during the appointment	• Is now excited to go to recess
• Enjoyed the car ride more and was patient during the ride	• Is trying new foods

Figure 4. Comments from Respondents

or ABA, design study was conducted in four preschoolers with autism. Of the four, three showed significant change in their targeted behavior, which can be attributed to reading the Sensory Stories.[4]

Case Example

As a student with autism, 6-year-old Stephen began the kindergarten year in an inclusive classroom. He was one of two students with a disability and was receiving a variety of special education services within the context of a regular kindergarten program. The transition from a structured special education preschool program to a regular kindergarten held many challenges for Stephen, one of which was the morning circle-time routine. Stephen preferred to move around the room, vocalize, and engage in repetitive movements. The behaviors disrupted the circle-time routine, causing education personnel to reconsider his inclusive placement.

Consulting with an occupational therapist, Stephen's classroom aide introduced and read the circle-time story to him on a daily basis. The story provided verbal reminders and physical cues to put his sock buddy in his lap, give himself a big hug, and rock slowly in the sitting position. Over a 2-month period, Stephen became able to sit through the course of the circle-time activity. His vocalizations, attempts to leave the situation, and repetitive movements decreased. Not only did the negative behaviors subside, but positive behaviors increased, as evidenced in his attempts to participate in the activity with the other children. Stephen successfully completed the kindergarten year along with his peers.

While several factors may have contributed to Stephen's improved participation in the circle-time activity, one factor appeared to be the regular reading of the circle-time story.

Conclusion

Occupational therapists who work with children with overresponsive sensory modulation disorders continually seek the best combination of programs to meet their needs. Sensory Stories are one more option available to consider. On the basis of the positive feedback to date, it is anticipated that many children, families, and teachers will come to understand sensory processing better and see a difference in occupational performance as a result of using Sensory Stories.

References

1. Ahn R, Miller L, Milberger S, McIntosh D. Prevalence of parent's perceptions of sensory processing disorders among kindergarten children. *Am J Occup Ther.* 2004;58:287–293.
2. Miller LJ, Reisman JE, McIntosh DN, Simon J. An ecological model of sensory modulation: performance of children with Fragile X syndrome, autistic disorder, attention-deficit/hyperactivity disorder, and sensory modulation dysfunction. In: Roley SS, Blanche EI, Schaaf RC, eds. *Sensory Integration in Diverse Populations.* Tucson, AZ: Therapy Skill Builders; 2001:57–82.
3. Marr D, Nackley V. Enhancing children's participation through Sensory Stories. Presented at: American Occupational Therapy Association Conference and Expo; April 2004; Minneapolis, MN.

4. Marr D, Mika H, Miraglia J, Roerig M, Sinnott R. The effects of Sensory Stories on targeted behaviors in preschool children with autism. *Phys Occup Ther Pediatr.* 2007;27(1):63–79.

5. Bandura A. *Social Learning Theory.* Englewood Cliffs, NJ: Prentice-Hall; 1977.

6. Barry L, Burlew S. Using social stories to teach choice and play skills to children with autism. *Focus Autism Other Dev Disabilities.* 2004;19(1):45–51.

7. Bruce M, Borg B. *Psychosocial Frames of Reference.* Thorofare, NJ: Slack; 2002.

8. Bundy A, Lane S, Murray E. *Sensory Integration: Theory and Practice.* 2nd ed. Philadelphia, PA: F.A. Davis; 2002.

9. Gray C. *Writing Social Stories with Carol Gray.* Arlington, TX: Future Horizons; 2000.

10. Scattone D, Wilczynski S, Edwards R, Rabian B. Decreasing disruptive behavior of children with autism using social stories. *J Autism Dev Disorders.* 2002;32(6):535–543.

Deborah Marr, ScD, OTR/L, and Victoria L. Nackley, MS, OTR/L, are the creators of Sensory Stories, available at www.theraproducts.com and www.sensorystories.com. Deborah is an associate professor of occupational therapy at Shenandoah University in Winchester, Virginia. She specializes in sensory processing, handwriting, and fine motor skills. Victoria is an assistant professor of occupational therapy at Utica College in Utica, New York. She specializes in sensory processing, motor learning, and early intervention.

Learning from Jean Ayres

Lawrene Kovalenko, MA, OTR/L

Do you have a child whose needs exhaust your coping skills? Is your child constantly derailed by things and events? Do your own unmet needs clamor, fill you with grief, or lay a pall on your spirit? I studied and worked with a woman who looked into such questions, and found some important answers. Jean Ayres was the Lance Armstrong of my profession, occupational therapy. In a series of upcoming articles, I'll introduce *S.I. Focus* readers to the groundbreaking work that she did and explain its relevance for today's children and families.

Dr Ayres' vision relies on knowledge about how brains learn. She graduated from the University of Southern California's School of Occupational Therapy in 1944 and was teaching their masters degree program in 1963 when I returned for an MA. Dr Ayres had figured out that a child's brain may be trying to kick-start itself, or self-repair, through behaviors that seem to be extreme, irrational, or oppositional to other people. Her information revolutionized my own self-understanding and changed my life.

I couldn't read or see numbers until after I was 12 years old. When my mother went to doctors for help, more than one of them got very angry with her. They said it was her fault. She had spoiled me rotten by reading out loud. Being read to had made me lazy. I was stubborn, demanding, and needed discipline, that's all. Doctors did not help with this problem.

For me, walking through the door of my schoolroom was walking into a place of blackness. I saw everything in the surrounding space of about two feet, that's all. Beyond that, opaque blackness went straight up and down to the floor; it surrounded me wherever I went. The blackness scared me at first, but I got used to anything that didn't change. My younger sister couldn't understand why I wasn't friendly to anyone in my class. She knew everyone. But I had no clue who anyone was for several years—teachers or kids. I didn't see or hear much of anything.

Starting in third grade, I stayed after school routinely twice a week. The deep sigh my teacher gave as she pulled up a chair to sit down remains an audible memory. She worked up a sweat trying to get me to pronounce words and understand math facts. I felt sorry for her. Different teachers tried, year after year, but nothing changed. When I got older I learned to look directly into a teacher's eyes and say, "It's not your fault."

Leaving school each day was walking out of blackness into daylight. Once home, I'd change my clothes and pretend to go outside. In fact, when no one could see, I'd quickly climb into the bottom of a laundry chute and pull the door closed. I'd discovered how to press my feet against one side of its smooth, cool metal, my back against the opposite side, and scoot up or down with ease. Inside was deliciously soundless and comforting. Soon pictures that were not about school rose in bubbles from somewhere. The reality of what was important to me drifted back and glued itself together. There was always a moment when something solid happened; I knew what I wanted to do and climbed out. Then I went outside. I have no idea how many months or years I did that, but it always worked.

I was over 30 and in graduate school when Jean Ayres asked, in a matter-of-fact voice, "Do you know how dyslexic you are?" The shock of her words turned my body into a kaleidoscope. Inside, below my neck, flat-surfaced, colored slabs slid and crashed around. I remember their sounds and an earthquake feeling.

That afternoon I got a pair of Zories (flat rubber sandals with one toe strap). My feet had to work every step to keep them on. For years I only wore Zories, never shoes. I bought flannel sheets and knobby towels, a back brush and loofa sponge. All of these gave me much-needed tactile input. I went to a nearby park and started swinging at top effort for at least an hour every day. I played with Dr Ayres' scooter boards whenever possible, and then made one of my own.

I don't know when the light went on inside my head, but it did. That term is not always a metaphor. It was a real experience of internal brightness that made everything in my mind appear clearer somehow.

Using the techniques I had learned made a huge difference in my life.

By the middle of the first semester, I was surprised at how easy reading and remembering had become. Nothing dramatic happened, but inside, a solidness grew that had not been there before. It's never gone away. That doesn't mean that I can spell or do math. But having what others call "a learning disability" is a nonissue.

Even if you haven't had the privilege of learning directly from Jean Ayres, you can benefit by reading her extraordinary book. Ayres writes clearly and with great thoroughness about perception and coordination problems that interfere with a child's ability to learn and be emotionally comfortable. *Sensory Integration and the Child* was written specifically for parents whose children have learning and behavior problems. It's a gold mine of relevant, essential information about a central dynamic of brain processing called *sensory integration*. Sensory integration is one of the coherence-generating activities that brains do. All parts of a brain that do sensory integration are places of multisense convergence, hubs of electrochemical data processing. They are working sites that are permanent and fixed anatomically, like big cities in a landscape.

Sensed information can be processed well or poorly through these areas. Sensory integrative dysfunction is the result of poorly processed information. What shows outwardly as a child's behavior is a child who cannot easily do what other children his age do automatically, without paying attention. Children with sensory integrative problems often need help learning how to do ordinary things. They may need help learning how to play, or make friends or get their hands to work together to stir something in a bowl, or draw with a crayon.

I want to urge all parents with special-needs children and anyone who works with these children to get a copy of the revised 2005 version of *Sensory Integration and the Child*. This new paperback changes nothing Jean Ayres wrote. It adds much-needed pictures and diagrams and an appendix of commentaries. Ten of the commentaries are written by clinicians, and one is written by Jean Ayres' nephew, Brian Irwin, and his wife, Christine Hunsicker. The book is a cornucopia of information, but don't expect to read it straight through like a story. It's a reference book and a textbook, as well as a scientifically accurate story about how brains develop and how brains teach themselves to learn.

I recommend that readers start slowly. Look through the book and at its pictures. Maybe read the forward by Florence Clark, and the story by Brian Irwin and Christine Hunsicker. Just reading those three pages will tell a reader volumes about the kind of person Jean Ayres was and why her potent intervention methods continue to be studied and used by an ever-growing number of practitioners. When you're ready, close the book and think about your own life. Think about the things your children do and things you yourself have experienced that may indicate the presence of some kind of sensory integrative dysfunction.

One way to flesh out a picture of possible problems, or syndromes, is to make a list—the more detailed the better—of each behavioral attribute of significance that your child does and that you feel yourself doing. What goes on, step by step, from waking up in the morning until going to sleep at night? What emotional state does each person in the household wake up in? What energy level? Remember that sleep deprivation alone produces toxic stress, which, when prolonged, saps energy and focus. Sleep deprivation is a weapon of intimidation when consciously imposed on a captive, is it not? Intensive research makes it clear that no human, indeed no vertebrate of any species escapes its debilitating effect.

Sleep and stress are not the only issues to sort out.

How do meals get made, and what happens during them? Each parent and each family member should make his or her own list without consulting others. There is no right or wrong attribute. The purpose of this activity is not to figure things out or come into agreement or learn to see "what's really happening." The reason for compiling such a list is discrimination and differentiation. Its job is to center each person in his or her own subjective truth of experience. It's about self-data gathering. Honesty and a willingness to release visceral truths to the waking mind are needed ingredients. Humor helps, as does inwardly directed good will.

Externally directed empathy, efforts at insight about others, or trying to be objective is counterproductive at this stage. A useful list anchors events into what happens where, when, and how often. Clock time and a sense of duration both matter. You may know something takes 10 minutes, but it seems like forever. That's important. You may sleep 6 hours a night, but it seems like 10 minutes. That's important.

When everyone is finished, comparing notes can be consciousness raising. Parents may be surprised at how differently each one experiences the same child's behavior. At that point, you might like to make a hierarchy-of-needs list. Prioritize changes both parents want and will cooperate to achieve. Below are some of the patterns to look for.

Feeling of "Overwhelm"

Overwhelm refers to being swamped. One can see fight-flight-freeze reactions. One child might respond to overwhelm with chronic weeping, another by staring into space, another by retreating to his room and playing video games for hours. Some children have meltdowns, tantrumlike fits of yelling, hitting, and kicking. Other children have flash fears. Their body contracts, they shriek and scream, and they can't stop. Meltdowns are exhausting. They show that something is "wrong," but not what.

Place and Situation

Places and situations that children fear tell a lot. Sometimes children will refuse to go into any sort of public bathroom. Sometimes a child will refuse to walk down one particular street, but not other streets. A child may be terrified by playgrounds or markets or movie theaters—places most kids love to go. I remember getting hysterical at the sight of mannequins, but I didn't mind stores without them. Stores were just stores to the big people in my life, so what was wrong? No one knew. It is very difficult to pinpoint exactly why certain things may disturb a particular child, but recognizing that they do and avoiding such places or situations will be helpful whether it makes sense to another person or not. Over time, perhaps certain reasons can be observed, such as the lighting, sounds, smells, amount of activity, or hundreds of other reasons that might resolve over time or through therapy.

Sensation-based Problems

Sensation-based problems involve lights, sounds, smells, motion, and textures. Almost anything can produce shudders of horror in one child and be craved like an addiction by another. I'll never forget the face of a mom sighing, "He can't tolerate the sound of someone breathing." Or the devotion of a dad who took it for granted that his son had to be strapped into a car seat and driven around for at least an hour every night to fall asleep.

What Is Avoided?

Remember to write down what your child does not do. Behaviors that are not expressed—by your child or yourself—may be harder to notice, but they tell just as much. Does your child just never want to get dirty? Does he avoid playing with big toys but likes to play with little miniscule things—or visa versa? Is your child attracted to hammers or baseball bats or anything that can be used to hit other objects, but refuses to learn to cut with scissors or to play with yarn? Are certain foods, food textures, temperatures, or tastes categorically rejected? Sensory integrative problems have enormous range and diversity. That's why making your own list about what is going on is so useful.

    If you suspect your child has a sensory integrative problem, the next step, after listing what happens, is finding an experienced therapist trained in Ayres' approach. Words like *sensory integration, sensory processing, sensory diet,* and *functional skills* are in the public domain and mean different things to different people. Their fluid use in conversation or written report is no indication a person knows anything about Ayres' work.

Take the time to find the right person. Ask around, do research, and find someone who is trained in Ayres' approach to evaluation and treatment. Not all skilled clinicians administer her Sensory Integration and Praxis Test, or SIPT, but all of them should understand the meaning of SIPT results. Clinicians evaluate sensory integrative problems in a number of ways. The goal is finding someone skilled in the remediation of characteristic, dysfunctional syndromes.

The way a sensory integration clinic looks and feels is important. You should find a reasonably large space with hanging equipment and mats on the floor. You should meet a person who welcomes questions and enjoys explaining to parents what you can do specifically to help your child. Once you've gotten that far and can locate your child's problems in the context of *Sensory Integration and the Child,* the book as a resource starts to grow.

Lawrene Kovalenko, MA, OTR/L, lives and works in Washington state. She currently serves on the advisory board of the occupational therapy department at the University of Southern California and works on collaborative efforts to provide education and occupational therapy services to critically underserved children with special needs and their families.

A Biomechanical Approach for the Improvement of Sensory, Motor, and Neurological Function in Individuals with Autistic Spectrum Disorder (ASD), Pervasive Developmental Delay (PDD), and Sensory Processing Disorder (SPD)

Charles W. Chapple, DC, FICPA

So frequently are behavioral and developmental disorders addressed through a variety of behavioral and chemical approaches that the significance of the biomechanical aspects of these conditions can be underestimated. This article introduces the importance of the nervous system with its biomechanical relationships to the spine and cranium and the noninvasive approaches of chiropractic and craniosacral therapy for the benefit of sensory, motor, and neurological function in individuals with autistic spectrum disorder (ASD), pervasive developmental delay (PDD), and sensory processing disorder (SPD).

As a parent of a toddler with ASD, PDD, and SPD diagnoses, I sympathize with other parents' drive to identify a cause and a solution. As a chiropractor with 14 years of experience and a fellowship in chiropractic pediatrics (and currently in pursuit of my certification in craniosacral therapy), I am additionally driven to identify a course of action that improves the structure and function of individuals with sensory, motor, and neurological dysfunction with these diagnoses. According to Sharon Rosenbloom, author of *Souls: Beneath and Beyond Autism*, speech and language pathologist, and mother with a son on the autistic spectrum, even the manual for diagnosis of individuals with ASD—the *Diagnostic and Statistical Manual of Mental Disorders,* or DSM—acknowledges mainly language, social, and behavioral variations, yet it minimizes sensory involvement. The recognition of the significance of sensory involvement with individuals with ASD, PDD, and dysfunction of sensory integration (DSI) diagnoses is the essence of realizing the significance of the nervous system. In persons with these special needs, an approach that naturally improves the body's structure or biomechanics is an essential component to their functional, educational, behavioral, and emotional development, as well as to their quality of life.

I have become aware of the many nuances and joys of viewing life through the eyes of a special-needs child. This experience has challenged me to further study and appreciate the significance of the body's most important organ system, the central nervous system.

The central nervous system is comprised of the brain and brain stem, the spinal cord, and the nerve attachments, which communicate with the body's cells, tissues, muscles, and organs. Within just 18 days of conception, it is the first body system to develop. It evolves to encompass a communication network of more than 45 miles of nerves, which sends vital messages between the brain and body at a rate of 325 mph. Within a 24-hour time frame, the communication of this system is responsible for more than (a) 103,000 heart beats, (b) pumping 2,100 gallons of blood, and (c) more than 23,000 breaths, thus exercising about 7 million brain cells.

The nervous system's importance to the body is highlighted by the fact that it is incased in protective bone—the brain by the skull and the spinal cord by the spinal column. Furthermore, fluid flow, which is affected by the relationship between the sutures of the bony skull and the sacrum, as well as receptor input at the joints of the bony spinal column, influence nervous system input. Therefore, improper biomechanics or body and/or bony mechanics can negatively affect the body's nervous system reception, which affects the body's sense of position (proprioception); motion, balance, muscle tone, coordination, motor planning, and auditory-language processing (vestibular sense); and touch perception (tactile sense), which is essential for academic learning, emotional security, and social skills. Even further reaching are the effects of poor mechanics on pain perception (nociception), as well as on many other body functions through the specialized communication of the autonomic portion of the nervous system. The 12 cranial nerves located at the brain stem are additionally significant to the body's effective and appropriate sense of smell, sight, taste, and hearing. This central nervous system and its intimately related bony protection system are a profound link between a person's external and internal environments, especially one with special needs. This link is critical in enabling a person to interact with his or her surroundings and others.

Healthcare practitioners are challenged to quantify variations of this vital communication with individuals diagnosed with ASD, PDD, and SPD. In fact, conventional neurological testing modalities, such as magnetic resonance imaging, or MRI; electroencephalography, or EEG; and varied genetic blood markers may commonly yield unremarkable results. However, in an effort to see the forest beyond the trees or to identify improvements to be made in the function of the nervous system beyond a diagnosis, noninvasive testing by means of infrared thermography and/or surface electromyography (EMG) can yield productive quantitative data.

Infrared thermography is used to measure the imbalances in temperature along the spine. Whenever communication between the central nervous system and blood vessels is malfunctioning as a result of subluxations, definable differences in temperature are identified by abnormal color patterns (Figures 1 and 2). Therefore, similar imbalances exist within the autonomic nervous system, which adversely affect organs and glands. Surface EMG is used to measure the effectiveness of motor nerves by measuring the amount of current located in the muscles. Subluxations disturb the operation of the motor nerve and are thus identified by abnormal color patterns produced by the surface EMG (see Figures 3, 4, and 5).

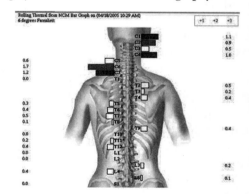

Figure 1. Rolling thermal image acquired before chiropractic adjustment.

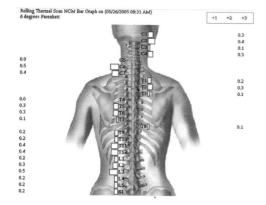

Rolling Thermal Scan NCM Bar Graph on (05/26/2005 09:31 AM)
6 degrees Farenheit

+1 +2 +3

Figure 2. Rolling thermal image acquired after chiropractic adjustment.

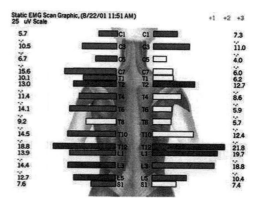

Static EMG Scan Graphic. (8/22/01 11:51 AM)
25 uV Scale

+1 +2 +3

Figure 3. Surface EMG image acquired before chiropractic adjustment.

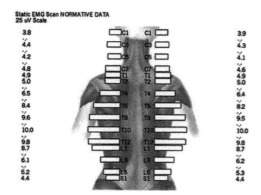

Static EMG Scan NORMATIVE DATA
25 uV Scale

Figure 4. Surface EMG image acquired after chiropractic adjustment.

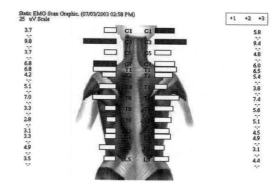

Static EMG Scan Graphic. (07/03/2003 02:58 PM)
25 uV Scale

+1 +2 +3

Figure 5. Optimal surface EMG image.

Chiropractors identify the need for, and utilize, gentle pressure techniques, called *adjustments*, to remove subluxations. Subluxations are characterized by *(1)* irregular bony mechanics or spinal misalignments, *(2)* nerve imbalances, *(3)* muscle irritation, *(4)* tissue inflammation, and *(5)* degenerative wear. The poor structure involved in a subluxation results in poor motor, sensory, and neurological function. An individual with subluxations may experience multiple health concerns, ranging from (but not limited to) pain, asthma, bed-wetting, digestive upset, neurological disorganization, attention deficit and/or hyperactivity, scoliosis, and spinal degeneration.

To an individual with ASD, PDD, and/or DSI, subluxations could additionally manifest in numerous forms, possibly accentuating a hypo- or hypersensitivity. Hyposensitivity is a symptom of a less-active sensory portion of the nervous system; in essence, the "volume" of sensation is turned down too low. Commonly, motor and other neurological functions are also hypoactive. Conversely, hypersensitivity is a symptom of an overactive sensory portion of the nervous system; the "volume" is turned up too high. A principle indication of hyposensitivity is a craving for a sensation of pressure, and a principle indication of hypersensitivity is the avoidance of pressure or touch. (Hypersensitive individuals can present their own set of challenges when utilizing a hands-on treatment, such as chiropractic or craniosacral therapy. Frequently, parents and siblings help in defining a comfort zone for the hypersensitive individual.)

A chiropractic adjustment restores more appropriate sensory, motor, and neurological input at the receptors of joints. Therefore, with either a hyposensitive or hypersensitive individual, one purpose of an adjustment is to "turn up" or "turn down" the "volume" of sensory input. It would then be reasonable for a parent or caregiver to note subjective gains, such as reduced sensory or motor stimulation, and for a chiropractor to document biomechanical improvements through reexamination or thermography and surface EMG.

Craniosacral therapy focuses on relieving undue pressure on the brain and spinal cord through light manual pressure at the cranium (skull) and sacrum (base of the spine). This craniosacral system is made up of the membranes and the cerebral spinal fluid, which serve to protect the central nervous system. Manually monitoring its rhythm allows detection of restrictions in this hydrostatic fluid system. As irregularities in cardiovascular and respiratory rhythm could indicate numerous health concerns, so, too, variations in the craniosacral rhythm could indicate any number of motor, sensory, or neurological impairments. A few examples of such conditions are migraines, chronic pain, fatigue, and learning disabilities. Similarly, following a course of craniosacral treatment, both subjective and objective references would be monitored for expected improvements. Craniosacral therapy practitioners are commonly massage therapists, chiropractors, osteopaths, and physical and occupational therapists. These healthcare providers may also pursue additional training in related techniques, such as lymphatic drainage.

Ultimately, a biomechanical approach to improve sensory, motor, and neurological function for these special-needs individuals can be enhanced by bioenergetic, biochemical and/or nutritional, and bioemotional components. Within this complementary approach, which would ideally involve many separate healthcare practitioners and approaches, a person's total health can be addressed. Furthermore, although chiropractic treatment and craniosacral therapy, either separately or shared, are not meant to be a cure for individuals with ASD, PDD, and/or SPD, functional, behavioral, emotional, and educational gains are legitimate goals whenever structure is improved and function follows.

Chiropractic physicians complete a postgraduate education similar to their medical colleagues but with less emphasis on pharmacology and surgery. A chiropractic education further emphasizes anatomy, neuroscience, diagnosis, pathology, radiology, and clinical nutrition. Once licensed, chiropractors may pursue certifications, fellowships, or diplomate programs, such as those in acupuncture, pediatrics, neurology, diagnosis, radiology, and sports.

To locate a chiropractic and/or craniosacral therapy practitioner who works with special-needs individuals, contact your state chiropractic, therapist, and autism associations or national organizations, such as Cure Autism Now. On the Internet, check *www.upledger.com* and *www.icpa4kids.com*. Furthermore, a book with an excellent resource section is *The Out-of- Sync Child,* by Carol Kranowitz.

Special acknowledgments to David Singer Enterprises, the Chiropractic Leadership Alliance, Dr Kevin Imhoff, and Ann, Sean, and Caitlyn Chapple.

References

1. Fysh PN. Upper respiratory infections in children: a chiropractic approach to management. *ICA Review.* 1990;March/April:29–31.

2. Kunert W. Functional disorders of internal organs due to vertebral lesions. Ciba Symposium. 1965;(3):13.

3. Peet JB. Subluxation detection in infants. *Today's Chiropractic.* 1990;February/March: 28–29.

4. Ressel O. *Kids-First: Health with No Interference.* Canada: New Century; 2000.

5. Rosenbloom S. *Souls: Beneath and Beyond Autism.* New York, NY: McGraw-Hill; 2004.

Charles W. Chapple, DC, FICPA, completed his undergraduate studies at Nazareth College of Rochester, NY, receiving a bachelor degree in biology before earning his doctorate degree in chiropractic medicine from the National College of Chiropractic in 1991. For more information, visit www.drchapple.com.

Research Review: Including Fathers of Children with Special Needs in Research Studies and Parent Support Programs

Jennifer Boothe Brobst, PhD; Kelly Davis, MA; James R. Clopton, PhD

To be a couple can be immensely gratifying, but it requires dedication, flexibility, and hard work. Couples who are also parents face added challenges as they work to balance their individual needs and preferences with their responsibilities to other family members. Children with developmental disorders, chronic medical illnesses, or other special needs present a variety of additional challenges to their parents and other relatives. The three of us conduct research and provide clinical services to children with developmental disorders and health problems. Providing effective services to these children requires efforts to assist parents, siblings, and other family members so that the entire family's quality of life is enhanced.[1] Here, we provide some background information from the research literature on families with children with developmental disorders or serious illnesses.[*] We also describe a special concern of ours—the relative absence both of fathers as participants in research studies and of support groups for parents of children with special needs.

In a previous article, two of us described both the positive and negative consequences that often occur when parents have children with special needs.[2] For example, these parents often are found to have higher levels of stress and depression, and they are more likely to divorce, although that added risk is lower than might be expected (3% to 6%). In contrast, some parents report no change in their marital relationships after the birth of a child with a disability, or they report positive outcomes, such as successful accommodation to the extra challenges and greater family cohesion. That contrast was also present in a comparison we made between 25 couples whose children have autism spectrum disorders and 20 couples whose children do not have any developmental disorders.[3] We found that parents of children with autism spectrum disorders experienced higher levels of parenting stress and less satisfaction in their relationships than the other group of parents, but they reported about the same level of some important resources for meeting those challenges (support from their partners, respect for their partners, and commitment to their marriages).

---

[*]For an extensive list of research studies used for this study, contact Jennifer Brobst, 18W100 22nd Street, Suite 130, Oakbrook Terrace, IL 60181; *jenniferbrobst@gmail.com*.

Our intent was to compare couples who were parents of children with autism spectrum disorders with couples who were parents of children who did not have developmental disorders. As it turned out, 90 parents (45 couples) and also some "uncoupled" parents—105 mothers and eight fathers—completed the measures for our study. However, most of the time, only one parent completed the measures (71.5%), and most parents who completed them were mothers (73.9%). Some who completed our measures were single parents. Most parents were given the measures while they were waiting for their child to be seen by a physician or other professional. Sometimes both parents, but more commonly only the mother, accompanied the child. When both parents were not available or did not have time to complete the measures before the child's appointment, the measures were sent home with a stamped return envelope to be completed later. Most measures that were sent home were not returned.

The fact that most of the parents who completed the measures for the Brobst et al study[3] were mothers is common.[†] Most participants in research studies of the parents of children with developmental disabilities, serious illnesses, or other special needs are mothers. For example, in a study of the parents of children in early childhood intervention programs, 64% of the participants were mothers, and 36% were fathers. A cross-cultural study of parents whose preschool children had disabilities and were attending early childhood programs demonstrated that the imbalance between mothers' and fathers' participation is not limited to the United States. Most participants in that study were mothers (over 80%), both in the United States and in Australia.

The proportions of mothers and fathers in those two studies were similar to that found in the study of Brobst et al,[3] but more extreme disparities can easily be found in research on parents of children with disabilities or serious illnesses. For example, nearly all participants in a mail study of parents of children with Fragile X syndrome were mothers (266 mothers and eight fathers). A similar disparity was found in an evaluation of a program in which parents of children with special health needs were matched on a one-to-one basis with trained parents whose children had similar conditions. In that qualitative study, 24 parents were interviewed by telephone, and even though the ratio of mothers to fathers was extreme (23 mothers and one father), it was representative of the overall rate of participation in the program. A review of research on children with serious illnesses found that 28% of the studies relied exclusively on mothers to report on the family's environment and on the adaptation of the child to serious illness.[4]

Although some of the studies in that review article justified relying solely on mothers because they are nearly always the primary care providers for children, it is more common for researchers to want to obtain information from both mothers and fathers. Therefore, it is important to consider several related questions: Why do fathers participate at a lower rate than mothers in research studies and parent support groups? In what way is that lower rate of participation a limitation? What might be done to encourage a more nearly equal rate of participation of fathers and mothers?

Little or no information is provided in most research studies about why fathers were less likely than mothers to have volunteered to participate. One study that did well in providing this information was a qualitative study of parents with children with Down syndrome who were in an early intervention program.[5] Two separate, simultaneous focus groups were conducted, one for fathers and one for mothers, and the style and content of those two groups differed. Having

---

[†]This phenomenon is not limited to parents. In a study that included individuals with disabilities, the family members of children with disabilities and of children who did not have disabilities, and professionals (service providers and administrators), 92% of the professionals who participated were women.

a child with Down syndrome increased the demands and overall stress level for mothers and fathers, but in different ways.

Mothers' stress was more related to the expectations they had for themselves in caring for their children, whereas fathers were more concerned about the "world outside their families," and fathers rarely talked about the pressure of taking care of their children's needs. Mothers more readily talked about their personal experience as the parents of children with disabilities. They were also more comfortable in asking for help from professionals and for support from other people and in interacting with the professionals who worked with their children.

Two special frustrations of fathers were identified in that study: (1) Fathers were surprised at how unhelpful and unavailable men in their extended families were in helping care for their children, whereas mothers reported receiving much help and support from women in their extended families. (2) Fathers were more likely than mothers to perceive negative responses to their children from other people.

Past research and our conversations with professionals who work with families whose children have special needs have suggested other reasons that fathers might participate less than mothers in research studies and parent support programs. Past research has shown that in response to disability or illness in their children, fathers are less involved than mothers with the care for children with special needs, and fathers are unlikely to respond with an expansion of their usual parenting responsibilities. Several professionals have told us of couples who respond to having a child with special needs by dividing the family responsibilities, with the mother becoming the main advocate and caretaker for the child and the father focusing on earning as much money as possible to pay for extra expenses. The income level of the family appears to have an enormous influence on the participation by parents in research studies and parent programs. In the study of Brobst et al,[3] most parents were college educated and had above-average incomes, and this feature is typical of other studies, as well. An indirect relationship between family income and father's participation was suggested by a study of parents of children with developmental disabilities. In that study, higher family income increased the marital satisfaction of fathers, which in turn increased their participation in child care. Fathers who are actively involved in caring for a child's special needs might participate more readily in research studies and in parent support groups because they may expect that those opportunities will be more relevant to what they are doing.

In seeking to involve the fathers of children with special needs in treatment planning, parent support groups, or research studies, professionals need to understand that mothers and fathers often respond differently to having a child with special needs. Furthermore, parents and professionals may have drastically different ideas about the family's needs. The parents' ideas may lead to behavior that professionals regard as uncooperative or resistant, so patience is required, as well as the determination to learn what parents truly need. For example, when the parents of children with Down syndrome were asked about their needs, both mothers and fathers emphasized the need to keep their marriages strong.[5] Whereas fathers also emphasized the need for couples to spend time with each other, mothers felt guilty about relying on others to care for their children while they worked or did something with their husbands. Perhaps fathers will become more involved in parent support groups if they know that such groups will focus not only on caring for the special needs of their children but also on the marital interaction of the parents. Although professionals should consider offering separate support groups for fathers because of the evidence that fathers appreciate the opportunity to receive support from other fathers,[5] fathers may not respond to that opportunity as quickly or as enthusiastically as mothers. Other suggestions for involving fathers include assuming that "fathers want to be involved" and offering services or conducting research studies at times that fathers are available, such as evenings and weekends.

In conclusion, the families of children with developmental disabilities, serious illnesses, or other types of special needs cope in a wide variety of ways with the challenges they face. The data in research studies show that parents whose circumstances are similar describe themselves in extremely different ways when responding to questionnaires or interviews. Some fathers of children with special needs attend parent support groups, take time off from work to learn more about their children's condition and its treatment, and are extremely involved in the daily care of their children. Nevertheless, the general pattern is for fathers to be less involved than mothers in childcare and less likely to participate in research studies and parent support groups.

We are not blaming fathers for not participating more than they do, nor blaming mothers and professionals for not doing more to encourage fathers' participation. Instead, we want to raise this issue to encourage discussion and creative problem solving. The relative lack of participation by fathers leaves all of us with an incomplete picture of how families adapt to having a child with special needs and limits our ability to design effective interventions and support services. Children with disabilities, illnesses, and other special needs will do best not only when they receive appropriate services, but when all members of their families are supported and assisted in having the best quality of life possible.

References

1. Shogren KA, Turnbull AP. Promoting self-determination in young children with disabilities: the critical role of families. *Infants Young Child.* 2006;19:338–352.

2. Boothe JL, Clopton JR. Research review: how parenting a child with special needs influences the marital relationship. *S.I. Focus.* 2005;Autumn:2-3,12–13.

3. Brobst JL, Clopton JR, Hendrick SS. Parenting children with autism spectrum disorders: the couple's relationship. *Focus Autism Other Dev Disabilities.* 2009;24:38–49.

4. Drotar D. Relating parent and family functioning to the psychological adjustment of children with chronic health conditions: what have we learned? What do we need to know? *J Pediatr Psychol.* 1997;22:149–165.

5. Pelchat D, Lefebvre H, Perreault M. Differences and similarities between mothers' and fathers' experiences of parenting a child with a disability. *J Child Health Care.* 2003;7:231–247.

Jennifer Boothe Brobst, PhD, is a clinical psychologist working in a group practice in a suburb of Chicago. Her interests include pervasive developmental disabilities, behavioral and emotional problems in childhood, and family coping strategies.

Kelly Davis, MA, is a graduate student in the clinical psychology doctoral program at Texas Tech University. Her research and clinical interests include familial relationships, coping, and youth internalizing problems in pediatric, maltreatment, and community populations.

James R. Clopton, PhD, is a professor in the clinical psychology program at Texas Tech University. His interests include research on eating disorders, consultation to community professionals and agencies, and the supervision of psychotherapy and psychological assessment. He recently coauthored the following article: Brobst JL, Clopton JR, Hendrick SS. Parenting children with autism spectrum disorders: the couple's relationship. Focus Autism Other Dev Disabilities. 2009;24:38-49.

How Captive Chimpanzees Help Us Understand Children with Sensory Integration Dysfunction

Elaine Jean Struthers, PhD, OTR/L

Being an animal behaviorist taught me the principles of sensory integration because every Wednesday I wore something like a spacesuit. I donned it after shedding my scrubs and showering. I wore double plastic gloves and booties, a bouffant cap, and a plastic face shield. Now I could enter the dull, windowless white room where six chimpanzees were living out their lives as human immunodeficiency virus, or HIV, research subjects. I really wanted to help these animals, who were contributing so much to human well-being. My mission was to find a way to enrich their environment and thereby decrease the "abnormal behaviors" they exhibited.

Once in the ward, I had difficulty because my suit deprived me of my senses. I couldn't feel anything I touched except in a large, lumpy way. My eyes kept focusing on a small scratch on the surface of the face shield, and this impaired my depth perception. Occasionally, I would kick over a bucket, and the contents swirled down a floor drain leaving a bleachy after-scent. The constant visual jockeying between the scratched shield and the vertical cage bars made me feel slightly dizzy and nauseous, and the smell of cleaning chemicals did not help. I was hot, too, and this was distracting me. I felt sweat pooling all over me, I was itchy, and I kept batting at myself to relieve this sensation. I could hardly hear anything, just the general roar of the air filter system followed by whispering rustles every time I moved in my plastic suit, and all of these sounds seemed to be coming from far away in the bottom of a barrel.

Every Wednesday, I took stock. I was in a room full of dangerous animals with my vision, hearing, and sense of physical self distorted. I was practically insensate, and I was alone. I never seemed to adjust. I wanted it to be Thursday, when I spent the mornings in the fresh air, watching happier chimpanzees jump, swing, and pull up dandelions in the outdoor play yards. (These days, whenever I meet a child with severe sensory dysfunction, I wonder if she feels like that: caught in a room full of dangerous others, alone and trying to use a body that just does not respond or react in a reliable or timely way. I always try to establish a sense of security with each child as a first step, for if she feels safe and trusting, then we can begin the important work of tuning-up the nervous system for better function.)

The chimpanzees in the ward rooms suffered from the symptoms of sensory deprivation. Some slapped, scratched, or bit themselves, some were pulling out their hair in large patches, a few rocked, banged their heads, or swayed incessantly, some repeatedly poked their eyes, and others simply lay about listlessly. All of these behaviors had been reported by different deprivation studies and researchers over many years.[1] Although we referred to these as "abnormal behaviors," I began to believe they were adaptations, perhaps even "normal" responses for individuals suffering from severe sensory deprivation.

I introduced a few simple enrichment approaches into the ward rooms, which reduced the incidents of hurtful behaviors. New behaviors began to appear, the chimps were glad to greet me, they laughed more often, and they tried to engage me in play by using toy objects I left in their cages. They ate with more gusto, vocalized with more enthusiasm and emotional range, and exhibited a greater interest in the world around them. I learned from this that when the nervous system is trying valiantly just to survive environmental conditions, little energy is left for simple pleasures, communication, play, and social engagement. Basic neurological sensorimotor needs must be met first, or more complex behaviors won't emerge.

Some things I did to improve the setting included painting one white wall a bright, glossy color. The goal was to add dimension and visual reference and to aid depth perception and orientation of self-to-environment. I used an aromatherapy atomizer in the air-intake system with garden scents unlikely to be noxious or introduce allergens, such as peppermint, marjoram, lemon, and basil. The goal was to change alert states, evoke emotional changes, and generally assist in internal state regulation. I introduced colorful toy objects and food puzzle boxes. The goal was to provide tactile variety and encourage longer periods of play with objects.

Finally, I used myself as a therapeutic object. I played games and introduced nonroutine, nonpredictable kinds of play. On Wednesday, I appeared with some new toy, food, or device. Some days I simply came with a notebook and took notes. The next week I might bring a bucket of bananas or giant blocks of ice with fruit frozen inside to be placed on the cage top so the chimpanzees had to climb up and, through the rungs, manipulate the ice to get the food out. Sometimes I held a game of tug-of-war with a dog's tug toy, pitting my measly strength against one chimpanzee while the others cheered us on. Sometimes I rolled in a television and played Jane Goodall movies. The chimpanzees all knew that once a week I would arrive, but they didn't know what I would bring with me. The goal was to have novelty within predictability, to add a time dimension and spontaneity to life. They learned pleasant anticipation, excitement, and reward, and later maintained memories and references to these experiences. Slowly but consistently, their hurtful behaviors began to disappear.

Chimpanzees taught me that we have to live in a world of neurological stimulation, or we will attempt to create it ourselves from whatever means are at hand. When I studied the different "abnormal" behaviors, I saw that they could each be tied to a central sensory pathway. Pressing the eyes triggered neural receptors, causing streams of neuroelectric stimuli to flood through the optical cortex. This could compensate for lack of visual input and interest in the environment. Swaying and rocking caused strong movement and vestibular sensations.[2] Such movement opportunities weren't available in a small cage, but the nervous system sought them, just as a hungry man seeks food. Pulling out hair stimulated dozens of touch sensors of various kinds. Self-biting stimulated oral-motor and deep-pressure sensation, also releasing opioid compounds[3] in the bloodstream that changed the way an individual felt inside. All of these self-created stimuli were a response to lack of opportunity and richness in the environment. Most of the hurtful behaviors could be mended through giving appropriate types and amounts of sensorimotor experience.

More recent research indicates that sensory deprivation can disrupt very specific processes that underlie learning and specialization or skill development.[4] We know that neurons in the brain itself cannot learn how to connect or grow in a purely physical sense if they do not receive environmental enrichment. The whole body-brain system *must* have sensorimotor "food" to produce patterns of neuron growth that lead to functional behavior. For instance, if we don't have auditory food we can't learn how to hear; without vestibular food, we can't learn how to move.

Sheila Hocken[5] writes in her book, *Emma & I*, that after she overcame blindness through surgery, a painting of the seaside on the hospital wall was only a meaningless blob of color to her. She had to learn how to see.

I was able to have one of my chimpanzee friends, Henry, relocated to a large indoor/outdoor cage with a nice tire swing in it after years spent in a 32-square-foot cage looking at the world through vertical silver bars, with no real vestibular-ocular "food." When Henry tried to jump off his perch to catch the swing, his timing and depth perception were so poor that he landed in a heap on the floor!

Both Sheila Hocken and Henry were able to quickly pick up the skills they needed through having experiences in their new sensory world. The brain literally restructured the dendritic connections and learned patterns of firing that allowed skills for movement and visual interpretation to emerge. I am convinced that there are other cases in which sensory deprivation is an innate characteristic of the brain, a result of an inability to properly process sensory and motor information from the outer world.

My experience in my protective spacesuit gave me a taste of what it might be like to be caught in a body-brain system that had severe sensory integration dysfunction. All of my sensorimotor reception was muffled, distorted, and inaccurate. I could perform gross movements but not refined ones. I could hear, but it seemed distant and dull. I could see, but my eyes kept darting around to things I did not want them to focus on. No wonder it was hard to move around without kicking things over. No wonder I felt frightened and alone. At least, as a "typically developed" adult, I had a basis for comparison. I knew there was a "normal" and reliable sensorimotor condition I would return to after removing all of my protective gear.

For a child with severe sensorimotor integration dysfunction, there is no basis of comparison. Every day may yield new and different sensory reception. Skills cannot be built on constantly changing and unreliable data about the environment. The person may be reduced to the most basic survival mode and filled with stress that can only be alleviated through what appear to be strange or hurtful behaviors.[3] These behaviors may actually be adaptive for the child. Part of our job as caregivers is to find an avenue to neurological enrichment that triggers sensory and motor reception and integration. Then the child can become more secure in his world, engage in functional activities, and build complex skills.

The challenge to caregivers of those who lack access to an enriched environment, either because of material circumstances or due to a particular diagnosis, is how to accommodate or remediate the condition. We can accommodate material circumstances by carefully planning opportunities and activities. Many children and inmates of various institutions, such as nursing homes, orphanages, prisons, and animal laboratories, will benefit from even simple enrichment strategies. We can remediate innate dysfunction by knowing the developmental sequence, understanding more about how the body-brain system works, and paying careful attention to the messages the person we are working with is giving us through his behavior. With or without a spacesuit, with or without caged chimpanzees, we can apply perception, empathy, and compassion to improve environmental opportunities for people with sensorimotor challenges.

References

1. Bowlby J. *A Secure Base: Parent-Child Attachment and Healthy Human Development.* New York, NY: Basic Books; 1988.
2. Ayres AJ. *Sensory Integration and Learning Disorders.* Los Angeles, CA: WPS; 1972.
3. Schulkin J. *Rethinking Homeostasis*. Cambridge, MA: MIT Press; 2003.

4. Zuo Y, Yang G, Kwon E, Gan WB. Long term sensory deprivation prevents dendritic spine loss in primary somatosensory cortex. *Nature*. 2005;436:261–265.

5. Hocken S. *Emma & I*. New York, NY: E.P. Dutton; 1978.

Elaine Jean Struthers, PhD, OTR/L, has spent 2 decades using sensorimotor techniques with captive nonhuman primates and children with autism spectrum disorders. Currently, she maintains a private pediatric practice and works at the Esperanza Clinic for Sensory Integration Dysfunction & Other Developmental Delays. She is available for consultation and presentations and may be reached through www.islandot.com.

Learning from Jean Ayres—Part 2

Lawrene Kovalenko, MA, OTR/L

The purpose of this article is to provide a sense of the experience two parents had when they took their 5-year-old son for an evaluation by an occupational therapist (OT) trained to administer Jean Ayres' Sensory Integration and Praxis Test, or SIPT.

Max's behavior was increasingly worrisome as he turned 5. His parents wondered what contributed to his incessant clamor for both emotional and physical help from his mother. Wanting her help from the moment he woke up until he finally fell asleep at night, he seemed to create "needs," one after another, to get it. For example, if his mother was in the garden, Max might climb up on something, then yell, "Mama, help me get down. You have to help me now!" Several other adults might also be there, but Max got hysterical if anyone else offered to help.

Parents and OT Discuss Max's Sensory Needs

The OT began by asking the parents about their greatest concerns regarding Max.

Dad: "Well, when his mother is anywhere around, Max just won't relate to me at all. He won't look at me or answer me. But if I'm the only one there, he's OK with me."

Mom: "That's true. Max physically hangs on me, or pushes on my face, or pulls on me. It's exhausting."

Dad: "He doesn't hang on me, but he tackles my legs. He pounds on me as if he wants to fight."

OT: "Yes. Max gets easily overwhelmed. He is only able to relate to one person at a time. When he first came into the clinic, he didn't speak to anyone, or look at anyone. Let's look at Max's SIPT results and see what's going on.

"Most of Max's skills are in the normal range, but a few are not, and that is really important. The first two items on the test are space visualization and figure-ground perception. Max has some strength in this area, but it's a double-edged sword. Doing a lot of visual imagery is a way to disconnect from one's body. Max can learn concepts visually, but he needs a lot of kinesthetic hands-on learning so that he can learn through his body.

"In the manual form-perception test, for example, I held up a folder so that he couldn't see what he was doing. Max did OK on this test, although he didn't like the loss of control. Then something happened that is important. It happened on other tests as well. When Max is done, he's done. He says, 'I'm done,' and stops. He won't engage again."

Dad: "He does that with me all the time. He wants to play ball, but after two or three throws he says, 'I'm done,' and just quits. He walks away on me."

Mom: "He does that with everything. We'll be having a conversation in the car, just Max and me, and suddenly it's, 'I don't want any more talking.' He gets really angry if I say anything after that."

OT: "Yes. Max's ability to persist and problem-solve isn't always there. The reason for this is that he isn't accessing all of his body's sensory information. It is a brain-processing issue, so it affects everything. He's not doing this on purpose."

Mom: "So how do you work with it?"

OT: "Well, if we can get his sensory systems more adaptable, so they don't shut down on him, it will help his ability to persist. This is the first test that didn't allow Max to use his vision, but he still cooperated. I know that if I'd come back to it another day he could have done more.

"He also continued to tackle the other tests, and he did fine until I drew shapes on his skin. Then he just couldn't get it. Max is a visually dependent kid. Even though his tactile system works pretty well, he overrides it with vision, so this means he doesn't always use touch sensations efficiently.

"The test Max scored really low on is praxis on verbal command. This test is about motor planning. When I told Max to put his elbows together, he put his knees together. When I told him to cross his legs and bend to the front, he bent to the side. I asked him to put one elbow on the back of his hand, and he put his elbow on his knee. I know Max knows the name of his body parts. This is about having an understanding of where one's body parts are in space and being able to translate verbal language—putting together the words he's hearing with the internal body sensations to do it.

"So Max is a child to whom you can't just give verbal directions. He needs a visual cue. You need to be right in front of him so that you know he is processing what you are saying.

"When he was in the playroom, for instance, and engaged with what he was doing, he wasn't processing verbal information at all. He didn't seem to hear anything that was said to him. How this problem affects his school experience this year may not show, because kids in kindergarten tend to get a lot of free time. If the teacher is giving verbal instruction, often the kids are sitting around her. But later on in higher grades, it really can be a problem, because a lot of teachers' instructions are verbal."

Mom: "OK, I understand that. What can we do at home?"

OT: "Well, for one thing, you can make pictures of the daily chores Max has to do. For example, if it's about cleaning his room, have one picture for each chore. One picture of where his clothes go. Another of where his cars and other toys go, another for the books, and so on. Place each chore to be done on a Velcro board; then Max can take it off when the chore is completed.

"This is also a way to teach sequencing. Max can see and learn the order in which to do things. Long-term, Max will probably be a fellow who makes lists, but he doesn't read yet, so you can make a picture of each task you want him to do. Start with only two or three steps, and place them in the right order. It really helps to get across the idea that routines have to be done every day, like getting ready for school, getting ready for bed, and so on.

"Max also has mixed results with other areas of motor planning; that's the praxis part of Dr Ayres' Sensory Integration and Praxis Tests. I sense Max is not putting together spatial information well, but I want to watch him do more spatial tasks. He shut down on the test that required building things with blocks, so I couldn't get information on what skills he might really have.

"Max started off doing OK copying body postures, but some were confusing for him. The one that involves crossing one's arms and putting one's hands on the opposite cheek was very confusing. It also took him a long time to figure out how to cross his arms and put his hands on the opposite knees."

Mom: "Are you talking about crossing the midline?"

OT: "Yes. Crossing the midline is subtle. You have to learn to see it. For example, when Max was putting shapes onto the form board, he always used his right hand. Always. That is a little too extreme. Max did well on the test, but he used his visual analytical skills. This is an example of why test scores alone can be tricky. It's not just doing something, but how it's done that matters.

"Here's another example. Max did OK balancing on a board, but he did it with lots of hand flapping. He does not do well standing still, so he hangs on you or leans on things. When he needs to stay upright on his own, he runs and uses momentum to give him a sense of body. He's a dynamic kid who wants to keep moving, but when he has to be still, he does not have good balance. And if his eyes are closed—forget it."

Dad: "Will horseback riding help with that?"

OT: "Horseback riding is excellent."

Dad: "We've just started horseback riding lessons, and we've been swimming, too."

OT: "Swimming is also excellent. Max has good upper extremity strength but surprisingly poor motor control in his hands. He can't use scissors, for example, and can't copy simple shapes. Some of this is visual-motor planning. He doesn't follow kinesthetically when he does things, so his pencil runs off the page. He doesn't end a motion when he needs to—we're back to momentum again. His brain is not spatially planning as his motor system does things. And he doesn't have a left-to-right orientation.

"Kids who are primarily visual processors don't do things in sequence, necessarily, so helping him learn to do things in sequence, like we've been talking about, will be really important."

Mom: "Are there games I can play with him that will help?"

OT: "Yes, lots. 'Simon Says' is a great one. Any game helps that involves one part of his body crossing to another side. Be as inventive as you can, but if you want help get the book, *The Out-of-Sync Child Has Fun*. That book has lots of ideas and you can look specific things up under specific categories, like crossing the midline. What Max does is use his cognitive thinking abilities to figure things out that his body should just quickly know how to do."

Mom: "Yes, I see him overriding stuff a lot. He stops to think about it."

OT: "I'm glad you said overriding, because that's what he does all the time. Max is a good thinker and he can analyze problems by thinking. But your body works most effectively when the lower part of the brain—the brain stem, cerebellum, and body sensations that feed them information—work automatically without thinking.

"If your brain isn't being used the way it's built to be used, it won't work well, and you'll be emotionally vulnerable and frustrated. So when you see Max doing something slowly, or responding with a slight lag, you're watching his override system taking over. He really needs to be able to respond to the world spontaneously and quickly. Games like 'Simon Says,' where you have to do things quickly, are great."

Dad: "We've just put up a cable between two trees. He's been asking for that.

Now he climbs a ladder and slides across the yard from one tree to another."

OT: "Wonderful! Anything that involves hanging, like monkey bars, or rings, or your slider, stretches muscles and joints and gives Max information from his body that he needs. Spinning in a swing is not so helpful—it can be too stimulating. What Max needs is to be grounded in his body by the information coming up to his brain."

OT Suggests OT and Sensory Integration

The OT summarized their hour-long conversation, ensuring that Max's parents understood the purpose and meaning of each part of Dr Ayres' SIPT. Then the OT recommended that Max start sensory integration therapy. She also reinforced the importance of their work with Max at home. Consistency at home is absolutely essential if a child is to make and sustain progress.

Clinicians who are trained to provide Ayres-based therapy work in a highly specialized environment. It is filled with equipment that people don't have at home, such as long tubes of stretchable material to crawl through, giant vats of balls, scooter boards and ramps to slide down, and various types of hanging platforms, nets, bolsters, and swings. Aryres therapists elicit behaviors that can't happen easily outside of a clinic and that challenge children in ways parents cannot.

Parents Relate Progress

The feedback parents get about change is subtle and not necessarily predictable. Positive changes are driven by experiences a child's brain seeks, and they don't take long to show up if the approach fits. When a child's brain starts to get the somatosensory information it needs, what that child does and wants to do alters, bit by bit.

The OT visited with Max's parents after 2 weeks of therapy and had this conversation:

Mom: "Did you know, Max asked if he could set the table? Set the table! I couldn't believe it, but he did."

Dad: "After his riding lesson, Max wanted to clean the horse's feet himself. He held the hoof in one hand and scraped it out carefully with the other. He was very gentle and thorough. Max cleaned all four hoofs. He did a great job. He didn't quit."

Mom: "Something is changing inside Max. He is doing things he never would have done before. Never. I just can't believe he wants to set the table now," she said, shaking her head, "but he does, every meal."

There is an OT principle called summation. That principle says, "Don't do just one thing at a time; do everything, and keep it up." It's the adding up of everything, the summation of all effort, that helps change happen. Along with consistency, a child needs continued challenges that are novel and get increasingly complex. Children's brains want to grow and master challenges and succeed. When given challenges that are "just right," children start to do things that give themselves satisfaction. They think up new things to try and practice on their own.

Lawrene Kovalenko, MA, OTR/L, lives and works in Washington state. She currently serves on the advisory board of the occupational therapy department at the University of Southern California and works on collaborative efforts to provide education and occupational therapy services to critically underserved children with special needs and their families.

Learning from Jean Ayres
—Part 3: A Passion
for Investigation

Lawrene Kovalenko, MA, OTR/L

Dr Jean Ayres' great genius, I believe, was a wholeness of clinical comprehension that allowed her to isolate age-specific abilities, which were both testable and amenable to remediation. She was the first psychologist with a PhD who created a specialized remedial environment (clinic space) that, when engaged, evoked behaviors that improved the deficits (the syndromes of sensory integrative dysfunction) her tests results demonstrated. In the 1950s and 60s, many neuroscientists and developmental theorists believed research on living systems in the process of dynamic function had too many variables for meaningful findings. However, it is time to recognize that Dr Jean Ayres' meticulous research on both evaluation tools and remediation techniques contained consistent, statistically reliable results.

By the 1960s, Ayres was gathering mountains of statistically significant evidence that children who couldn't learn—and were not emotionally and behaviorally self-contained—had anatomically definable areas in their brain stem and midbrain that were malfunctioning. Beyond that, her research on the effectiveness of specific remediation strategies showed that sensory integrative capacities, especially mastering the pull of gravity, sustaining focused attention, and becoming more self-directed, could be improved (Ayres, *Sensory Integration and the Child*). "A sensory integrative approach," wrote Ayres in 1972, "does not teach specific skills...the objective is the modification of the neurological dysfunction interfering with learning." Although improving specific skills, like handwriting, was never the goal of Ayres' remediation, it was a side effect. Additionally, many children became appropriately self-contained emotionally.

The prevailing world-view then assumed that children who were not learning and children with volatile emotions were being consciously resistive and oppositional. Conventional wisdom and the voices of powerful, persuasive, charismatic experts, like Melanie Klein, B. F. Skinner, and Milton Erickson, decreed that manipulative, defiant, uncooperative children had to be socialized and taught how to behave. Many who believed "bad children need to be socialized" began to develop therapies based on conditioning. According to Alice Miller, a German psychoanalyst and child advocate, all conditioning approaches share a central premise: It is the role and duty of a therapist to take action and to bring about change.

Miller calls this attitude "poisonous pedagogy." This form of pedagogy assumes willful intent on the part of the child, no matter what happens. A child who is out of control must learn to get himself under control, period. Such pedagogues find fault with any child who does not do what he is told, for any reason. It is this way of child rearing, which lingers to this day, that I believe caused Jean Ayres more grief and stress than anything a child ever did. For more than 30 years, she sustained focus that built not just a standardized test and two volumes of information, but also the legacy we have today: a system of standardized training that graduates nearly 300 clinicians a year.

Ayres' intention as a professionally trained occupational therapist was to evaluate and remediate physically disabling conditions. Facts she found significant were things like whether or not a child's eyes converged and tracked (worked together). Ayres didn't see laziness when a child fumbled with shoelaces instead of tying them; she saw poor coordination and an inability to motor-plan. She also knew how emotionally vulnerable children were, how they were filled with shame if their bodies didn't work as they should, if they could not skip rope, or play hop scotch, or cut with scissors, or fasten buttons, or make shapes out of clay, or go to the bathroom alone because they were scared of getting lost.

Ayres' effect on her profession was not subtle. It was as powerful and reorganizing as the effect her remediation techniques had on sensory integrative dysfunction in a child's central nervous system. If you dive with me into a time tunnel that goes back 43 years, we'll emerge in front of a weathered, two-story wood building on the campus of the University of Southern California (USC) in the middle of Los Angeles. It's the end of a hot, dry summer in 1962. Fourteen women from different parts of the country and different areas of practice are meeting here, the home of both USC's occupational therapy and physical therapy departments, for a year-long master's program, with the stated objective of teaching participants how to research.

It is a rare moment: Two equally brilliant clinical educators will convey very different kinds of information. Jean Ayres, a psychologist with a PhD, will provide two semesters of technical education and hands-on training, then leave for 2 years of postdoctoral work at the University of California, Los Angeles's Brain Institute. Dr Mary Reilly will pick up where Dr Ayres leaves off. The significant thing about Dr Reilly, if one focuses on sensory integration issues, is that her witty, profound, dazzling insights emerge from a brain that seems unaware it ever owned a body. Dr Reilly drives a car safely, but it is not safe for her to mix a salad. In half a minute, salad bits are all across the room and the bowl is empty, according to one of her friends. Dr Reilly is living proof that being dyspraxic and uncoordinated does not indicate low intelligence or an inability to learn, think, strategize, and problem-solve with great aplomb.

Back then, our class seemed large, though it was small and intimate by today's standards. We got to know one another very well because Jean Ayres' educational style was intense, hands-on immersion learning. All of us were experienced clinicians, reflecting diverse areas of occupational therapy knowledge and expertise. My clinical specialty was adult psychiatry. Several worked with children in hospitals. One specialized in infants at risk and made home visits. Another worked with teenagers at a school. All of us knew by then that Ayres' information about sensory integration and the effect of sensory experience on conscious attention, as well as on motor output, had relevance for every area of clinical practice. Ayres' information and concerns were rooted in the bedrock of occupational therapy's traditional role and contribution to the entire field of remediation.

I was always puzzled by Ayres' specific fixation on sensory integration. She acknowledged, but did not research, any other kind of integrative action the nervous system performs. Moreover, Ayres emphatically isolated the sensory integration mechanics involved with perceiving, engaging in, and manipulating the outer environment. Why was she so incredibly specific? That puzzle only resolved recently, after I found a book called *The Second Brain* (1998) by Michael Gershon, MD, and read what he had to say about the physiologist J. N. Langley, someone whose work Ayres also refers to.

Gershon says, "Langley remains the single individual most responsible for our current understanding of the autonomic nervous system." He explains further that there is an anatomical and functional difference between motor nerves and those of the autonomic nervous system. "Another system of motor nerves controls the behavior of skeletal muscles, which are usually operated voluntarily. This system is called the skeletal motor system…there are major anatomical differences between the nerves that go to the skeletal muscles and autonomic nerves." He describes the direct lines of motor nerves as information cables linking target areas in the brain with motor neurons and muscles. "A signal leaving the central nervous system en route to a skeletal muscle gets there intact and unchanged or it is not received at all." The same might be said about sense-specific nerve lines that transmit data from end-organ receptors (data recognition and capture) to the brain's primary and secondary cortices. "In contrast, an equivalent signal leaving the central nervous system en route to a blood vessel, the heart, or a gland may be amplified, weakened, or otherwise modulated by processes that occur at the autonomic synapses (junctions)."

"The activation of autonomic effectors thus is infinitely more subtle than that of skeletal muscles…this subtlety in the autonomic nervous system reaches a crescendo in the bowel." Autonomic nerve paths are always interrupted, Gershon says, or complicated by a multiplicity of co-existing factors and influences. The signals between brain and skeletal muscles, of a yes-no, on-off, working–not working nature, are simple and direct by comparison. Ayres would have also learned from Langley about the digestive system's powerful one-way effect, its upward influence on consciousness and sensory-emotional states, as well as its relative independence and autonomy. She would have known that the visceral brain's behavior—what our digestive system does and how it reacts—is affected very little by voluntary efforts to gain influence over what it is doing. In contrast, she also knew there were many avenues of access to the brain-muscle system, the perceptual-motor system involved with locomotion and hand-eye coordination that she worked with every day as a clinician. It is basic occupational therapy to understand that volition, will, intention, conscious focus, training, practice, and just plain wanting to improve send strong down-flowing signals to the musculoskeletal system and facilitate the sensory feedback that returns to the brain and motor command-control centers.

Although Jean Ayres graduated as an Occupational Therapist Registered, or OTR, in 1944, we can pick up the trail she both created and followed in 1954, with the last sentence of her master's thesis, "Proprioceptive Facilitation Elicited through the Upper Extremities." It says: "The greatest need [now] is to accumulate sound objective data that will aid in understanding the integrative action of the nervous system." Did Langley's information help Ayres identify the importance of sensory integration as something distinct, one of many kinds of sorting and processing dynamics the central nervous system did? We'll never know, but that speculation helped me follow the thread of seeking, experimenting, and validating that seems to have organized the trajectory of her entire professional life. After completing her master of arts thesis, Jean Ayres would tap everything she knew about helping a brain gain motor control over its own skeletal muscles when she became chair of a large occupational therapy rehabilitation clinic in one of Kabat Kaiser's active, innovative orthopedic hospitals. The job gave her access to updated medical research on nerve regeneration, muscle enervation, and the latest remediation techniques. She would have continued to learn about the importance of patients' conscious investment in what they were doing and the power of excitement about skills that could be improved.

The responsibilities and workload Ayres had on that job boggles my mind, whereas her mind thrived. On top of clinical, administrative, and teaching responsibilities, a 3-month-long training course ran a continuous cycle. Ayres gathered and organized as much information as she could about how the nervous system grows and develops, motor reflexes, the basic laws of kinetic movement, how a person's gait and the play of synergic muscle groups change with speed, the effects of weight or load on reflex activity, how reflexes affect one other and affect muscle tone, and more. The clinical responsibilities of that setting required occupational therapists to devise projects that were closer to everyday tasks than strength-building exercises. Projects needed to evoke emotional investment, the "I want to do it" drive that sustains attention. Ayres understood the need for success. To experience failure after failure has its own negative conditioning effect. Constant failure makes things worse. Being punished for failing makes things worse. A therapist's task is to provide tasks that challenge a person and that require effort but that can be accomplished. Being occupied in doing such tasks is self-rewarding and keeps a person engaged with the process of his or her own remediation. In 1958, Ayres published a paper called, "Basic Concepts of Clinical Practice in Physical Disabilities." Its stated intention was to "help clarify and encourage the growth of the fundamental theoretical foundations which underlie the treatment of physical disabilities through occupation." The first paragraph states, "a commonly accepted justification for the use of crafts and games as therapeutic media is their emotional value. This reason is accepted as a basic and important assumption empirically, but not scientifically demonstrated."

In 1958, and to this day, no one wanted to hear that they needed to prove scientifically that play was valuable to use it therapeutically, with children or anyone else. Some felt personally accused of being less than professional if they didn't want to research what they were doing or couldn't figure out how to. Being good at generating research is a unique talent, unrelated to, and not always fused with, the talent of being a skilled clinician. Ayres was not unique, but she was rare in having a talent for both. No other department chair, before or after Ayres, would have the same passion, the same need to investigate the role of sensory integration; every clinician must follow his or her own interests, and each one contributes differently to the growing body of knowledge in any profession. Ayres' imperative went beyond what was required to run that department, educate new students, and provide quality care to patients. But she certainly didn't invent the idea that it was mandatory to test, measure, evaluate, and record just about every definable aspect of a person's physically disabling condition. That was part of her job. It was also part of her job to test, measure, evaluate, and record the progress of remediation—or the lack of it.

What startled people, I think, was her ability to transfer the same strict clinical criteria to a new population with unexplored problems. But Jean Ayres was a scientist by nature. Her brain approached problems by asking questions, generating research, analyzing the results, and coming up with new questions. She settled for nothing less than valid, reliable, statistically significant information. "The only way I can teach you about research," Ayres said to the class, "is to show you what I did and where I got started."

Lawrene Kovalenko, MA, OTR/L, lives and works in Washington state. She currently serves on the advisory board of the occupational therapy department at the University of Southern California and works on collaborative efforts to provide education and occupational therapy services to critically underserved children with special needs and their families.

Learning from Jean Ayres—Part 4: The Developmental Sequence

Lawrene Kovalenko, MA, OTR/L

Jean Ayres' research on syndromes of sensory integrative dysfunction focused on children at school. If a child's developmental issues can be addressed before the challenges of school pile up, then the start of school is too long to wait.

One of the most important aspects of parenting is understanding the developmental sequence: the growth and development of sensory, motor, and perceptual systems that register and synthesize data from our physical bodies and outer environment. These systems enable us to move intentionally and interact effectively with people and things in our environment. To allow development and daily life in general to proceed "normally," these systems must receive precise, simultaneous, and continual flow to all integrative centers of the central nervous system. At any time after conception, components of a child's individual developmental potential can fail to express fully or can develop in atypical ways.

Many motor behaviors represent early developmental markers. They are evidence of skills being acquired and, if missing, signal possible delay and the possibility of problems in the future. Markers are significant, and it helps for parents to recognize them. The first article in this series (published in autumn 2005) reminded readers that a challenge parents face if they think a child may have sensory integrative problems is learning to see what that child is *not* doing, learning to notice what's missing. What a child does *not* do, has never done, and avoids doing may have important future consequences.

Masking Problems with Compensatory Adaptation

Every life form—plant, animal, fish, insect, or human—expresses unique developmental sequences and life cycle. Likewise, each functional system in the body is specialized to do unique tasks that no other can do. A brain's efficiency is genetically built to depend on and expect accurate information from all of its functional systems. What is understood now is that if one area of development or even an entire system fails in expression, the speed of overall growth and change continues at a pace that is species-specific. Decisions are constantly being made at electrochemical speeds and automatically compensate for deficits by using what has already been expressed and is working. This is called compensatory adaptation and can mask problems for a while.

Think of our brain's deep problem solver as Scotty in "Star Trek" and the conscious mind (forebrain circuitries), the source of conscious choices, as Captain Kirk. Scotty works deep in the hold of the ship's mechanical center. He receives "commands" from Kirk and must get the Enterprise, our neuromuscular physiology, to do whatever Captain Kirk wants. The ship's ability to move through space and respond appropriately to novel and extreme situations relies on the accuracy of its many data collectors, our sensory systems. They all work continually and their information fluctuates, depending on what the ship is doing and needs to do next. Down in the hold, Scotty must understand what the fluctuation of dials and data banks means. He is instantly alerted if information about structural stress, temperature, or gaseous build-up is missing or represented inaccurately. Facts about the outer environment are as essential as facts about the ship's internal environment.

We know it's Scotty's brilliance at jimmy-rigging and fast, adaptive problem solving that often gets the crew out of life-threatening crises. Just as Kirk doesn't know what Scotty does to keep the ship running, a child is not aware of his brain's adaptations, though he is aware of feeling anxious, fearful, and desperate or happy, excited, and relieved, and those feelings directly affect his behavior and conscious choices.

In article two of this series (published in winter 2006), an occupational therapist reminded the parents of 5-year-old Max how vulnerable their boy felt because the lower, sensory-integrative centers of his brain (brain stem and cerebellum) weren't getting the information from his body that they needed. In Max's case, the inadequacy was data from his muscles (proprioception). His brain had poor understanding of where his limbs were and what they were doing.

Understanding a Child's Internal Conditions

Unlike the "Star Trek" scenario, when a child's internal conditions can't self-correct, he or she behaves in ways that force others to pay attention and/or impose limits from the outside. If your baby yells, kicks, throws things, and cries whenever he's taken to a restaurant or market or on an airplane flight, you will not want to take him "out" very often. However, if parents understand sensory overload, they can learn to detect sounds, movements, smells, lights, and other conditions in the environment that their child can't tolerate. This knowledge helps them learn to avoid certain environments, if possible, as well as learning calming techniques like swaddling (wrapping an infant tightly and firmly), rocking, deep-pressure hugs, and soft rhythmic singing.

Parents with these vulnerable children may tend to organize their lives around emotional behaviors and clamoring needs that stay immature and don't resolve with time, but instead become entrenched. What does grow rapidly and with increasing complexity is a child's skill at manipulating his environment. It's virtually impossible for parents in this predicament to identify missing or dysfunctional developmental steps without guidelines, objectives, and comparative information.

Picturing the Developmental Sequence

At last, the developmental sequence is being intensely researched, and books about that research are starting to be published. One of the most recognizable "skipped steps" involves the drive to walk and the refusal to crawl. Another skipped step, the lack of seeking eye contact and not mirroring an adult's facial expressions, is so important that this theme will continue in the next article. Disinterest in play with other children is another, and this is also a huge topic. There are many others, including fear of movement or the opposite. I have roamed scores of bookstores to find material that is presented usefully for parents. Such books are quite scarce; however, Lois Bly's *Motor Skill Acquisition in the First Year*[1] is a beautifully photographed picture book, with thoroughness and attention to clinical detail that is an enormous contribution to the field of child development.

Bly is a physical therapist and kinesiologist. She writes for clinicians, but don't worry about the technical data—just look at her pictures carefully. They contain a lot of developmental information, more than the written text discusses. There is no faster way to learn what the developmental sequence is all about than seeing pictures of it in action. Another reason I recommend Bly's photographic information is that most of us have a need to visually study something we're learning and thinking about. Her pictured steps are detailed enough that a reader might discover that his child has never done some of them.

Using—and Growing—Sensorimotor Systems

The neuroanatomy of sensorimotor systems grows from being used. Its existence is activity dependent. Each stage builds new complexity from what is already there. By third or fourth grade, pressures to process greater volumes of information and solve increasingly complex problems start to mount exponentially. Compensatory adaptations that worked when the child was 3 become increasingly problematic.

For example, at the age of 5 (preschool), Max was overly dependent on seeing and thinking because his body was not able to perform motor-planning tasks quickly and automatically. Now that he is getting Ayres-based remediation weekly to address his sensorimotor deficits, Max will be more able to learn not only in elementary school, but also later, in middle school, where the academic and social pressures intensify.

Applying Four Generalizations to the Developmental Sequence

The developmental sequence has many steps and stages; four generalizations can be applied to developmental processes:

1. There are clear ages when specific motor skills emerge. Emerging motor skills must be practiced until they become automatic.

2. There are countless specific sequences to track, all of them moving from simple to increasingly complex. For example, your baby must learn to roll himself over and stabilize his trunk (middle body) before he can learn to stand and walk. The muscles of his head, neck, and shoulders must learn to keep his head stable on a neck and shoulders that continually move. His muscles must learn to hold his eyes horizontal (level with the horizon) before his visual cortex can accurately learn to perceive vertical and horizontal edges or the direction that objects are moving relative to him.

3. There is age-dependent plasticity, which refers to the ease of learning at an early age versus the difficulty of learning later, in some areas. A number of culturally specific behaviors, such as understanding and speaking a new language, get increasingly harder to learn

as a child ages. This is especially true after puberty. Age-dependent plasticity makes it hard for many adults to change cultures or learn motor skills they have never seen or practiced while growing up.

4. Growth happens in surges, followed by periods of rest. Some critical periods of change involve stress, and that stress seems to catalyze internal reorganization and the rapid development of new abilities. A classic example of stress catalyzing adaptation is birth itself.

Bonding and the Sensorimotor System

Wenda Trevathan is a physical anthropologist, whose seminal research on birth and parent-child bonding is described in her book, *Human Birth: An Evolutionary Perspective*.[2] Trevathan describes a variety of early "critical periods." She says that the first hour after birth is important for the infant in many ways but is "a relatively unimportant period in the mother-infant bonding process." According to Trevathan, in humans, the "maternal sensitive period" lasts from a few hours to 3 days after birth, during which "the mother is most sensitive to her infant and bonding takes place most readily" (p. 208).

"There is a definite progression and an orderly sequence in the nature and amount of contact a mother makes with her child. Instead of licking their young, human mothers make extensive use of their hands in immediate interaction with their infant" (p. 151). She describes the importance of a mother's initial fingertip exploration and palm contact with a newborn's skin. Skin-to-skin contact is a simultaneous, interactive exploration of each other that includes kissing, hugging, and smelling, as well as close, sustained eye contact (mutual gaze), vocalization, and nursing (p. 206).

Trevathan describes a number of mutual experiences that influence bonding and help the full capacity of a neonate's sensorimotor and perceptual systems to develop easily and with "normal" speed. They enhance survival and stimulate further social interaction, as well as develop the mother-infant bond (p. 149). These postural-based motor behaviors flow reciprocally and unconsciously between an infant and mother, an extension of the interactive synchrony that existed in utero. These include rhythmic movements, sounds, and continual bodily readjustments that remain synchronous in and out of sleep-wake states. Trevathan states that this reciprocal entrainment is "extremely significant" (p. 176) to the developmental process.

Imagine for a moment the experience of a new mother whose newborn arches backward and screams when he's touched. What if he turns his face away whenever she leans close and then won't make eye contact? What if he refuses to nurse? Full breasts are painful, but no pain matches the grief and heartbreak this primal rejection creates. It shatters a mother's world. Trevathan reminds her readers that developmental experiences are, by nature, mutual and simultaneous. An infant whose body can't integrate the tactile aspect of expressed love or express the motor aspect of mirrored, reciprocal emotions also feels primal isolation, despair, fear, grief, and loss.

The sensations that accompany grief and loss won't let up. These, like those of all emotional states, don't originate from the same sensory substrate Ayres researched, nor can the tools that remediate sensory integrative dysfunction mitigate their intensity. But Ayres is extremely aware of bonding issues and writes about their disruption, especially in her chapter on tactile defensiveness.

Evaluating a Child's Development

Nothing is more stressful than worry about a child who is obviously upset or withdrawn or who cries day after day. When all is said and done, the most critical and furthering thing parents can do is have their child evaluated by a professional with expertise in child development, someone knowledgeable about the type of problem they have noticed in their child. It requires searching, but don't give up. When you find the right person, or group of professionals, you and your child may acquire a team—a pediatrician, a behavioral optometrist, a speech and language therapist, an occupational or physical therapist, and one or more teachers.

Every child, family system, and community is unique, and real help can show up in surprising ways. The point is, as parents, you also need help and supportive collaboration, just as your child needs one or more accurate evaluations and appropriate, effective intervention. Different areas of a problem may require different types of remediation, but when intervention is effective, the results are obvious.

Coming Up: Instinctive Remediation

This article has just scratched the surface of information about the developmental sequence. The next will introduce Ayres' approach to remediation and the role of mirror neurons and will tell the story of a grandmother who spontaneously did something with her 4½-month-old grandson that could be seen as a classic Ayres remediation remedy. The grandmother was unaware of Ayres' work. Her behavior was operant and instinctive. Learning to recognize the remediation in parental instincts is another facet of learning for parents of children with sensory integration problems. In addition to bringing your attention to worthwhile resources and affirming the value of trained professionals, I look forward to sharing my first-hand observations of instinctual behavior as a family dynamic.

References

1. Bly L. *Motor Skill Acquisition in the First Year.* San Antonio, TX: Therapy Skill Builders; 1994.

2. Trevathan W. *Human Birth: An Evolutionary Perspective.* New York, NY: Aldine de Gruyter; 1987.

Lawrene Kovalenko, MA, OTR/L, lives and works in Washington state. She currently serves on the advisory board of the occupational therapy department at the University of Southern California and works on collaborative efforts to provide education and occupational therapy services to critically underserved children with special needs and their families.

Making the Connection between Primitive Reflexes, Sensory Processing Disorder, and Chiropractic Solutions

Charles W. Chapple, DC, FICPA

Sensory processing disorders encompass any condition that demonstrates the inability to process information through the senses. Any person who has spent quality time with an individual diagnosed with sensory processing disorder (SPD), autistic spectrum disorder (ASD), attention-deficit disorders (ADDs) (eg, attention-deficit/hyperactivity disorder, or ADHD), and pervasive developmental delay (PDD) acknowledges the presence of irregularities in sensory processing. Whether it be rocking, heightened impulsiveness, awkward balance, or an aversion to or a fixation on a noise or an object, at its core is the ineffective communication between internal and external environments.

Understanding the nervous system helps the parent and practitioner to find solutions. Acknowledging and evaluating persistent primitive reflexes or retained primitive reflexes (RPRs) and their relationship to the nervous system, along with their effect on sensory processing, can be a critical aspect of diagnosis, cause, and treatment for these individuals.

An equally integrated function of the central nervous system (CNS) is the body's interpretation and application from the senses, as well as its transition from the primitive reflexes seen in the newborn, such as the "sword fighter's stance," to the more mature postural reflexes of the older infant and toddler, such as protective movements that maintain safety and balance. Our "far senses" respond to a stimulus outside of our bodies. These senses allow interactions with what we hear, taste, touch, smell, and feel. Our "near senses" or "hidden senses" automatically respond to a stimulus within our bodies. These senses enable body awareness and balance. Our primitive reflexes and sensory systems facilitate our first interactions of life.

Primitive reflexes are automatic survival responses to stimuli, which develop during uterine life and should be fully present at birth (see Figure). These reflexes are typically inhibited by the higher brain in the first 6–12 months of postnatal life. These higher brain centers regulate postural reflexes, which are involved in voluntary and developmental movement. In essence, gross motor development must precede fine motor development, which fosters an ordered learning. From primitive to postural reflexes, to subsequent motor patterns, to perception, to language, to awareness, and then to academics, a learning "hierarchy" is to be built.

71

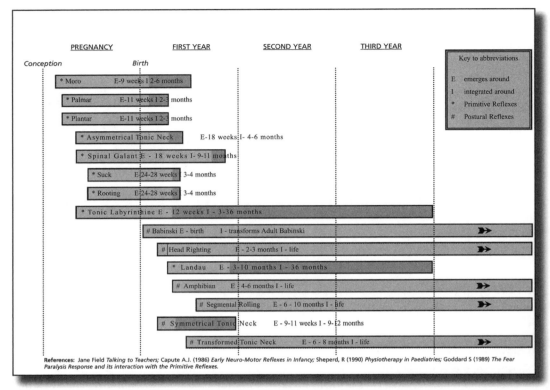

Figure. Approximate emergence and duration of primitive and postural reflexes.

RPRs are reflexes that have remained when the postural reflexes do not fully develop. Therefore, the body remains under the influence of the involuntary instead of voluntary control. RPRs have been related to difficulty with movement and balance, irregular visual and auditory perception, and irregular sensory processing. Subsequently, an individual with RPRs could appear clumsy, have difficulty utilizing both sides of the body for a task, and have poor visual tracking and judgment, as well as attention, behavioral, and socialization difficulties.

The role of the CNS is to sort through this maze of neurological impulses and route them to the correct destinations. Although no health care is guaranteed or without risk, chiropractic and craniosacral therapy can be a safe, noninvasive, and effective way to improve the CNS's supportive structure and therefore enhance its function. Chiropractic and craniosacral therapy may be beneficial in improving the integration of RPRs into the more developmentally mature postural responses, allowing the child to experience improved movement and sensory function.

An individual is defined as having problems with sensory processing concerns when he exhibits variations in frequency, intensity, and/or duration of sensory activity. The effects of these variations are seen as underresponsivity and overresponsivity. An individual with SPD, ASD, ADD, ADHD, or PDD, as well as other CNS imbalances, may experience a worsening of symptoms of these conditions as a result of subluxations. Subluxations are characterized by *(1)* irregular bony mechanics of spinal misalignments, *(2)* nerve imbalances, *(3)* muscle irritation, *(4)* tissue inflammation, and *(5)* degenerative wear. Subluxation results in poor motor, sensory, and neurological function. Additional challenges might manifest in numerous forms, possibly accentuating an underresponsivity or overresponsivity.

Ultimately, a biomechanical approach to facilitate reflex, sensory, motor, and neurological function for these special-needs individuals can be benefited by bioenergetic, biochemical and/or nutritional, and bioemotional components. Within this complementary approach, which would ideally involve many separate healthcare practitioners and approaches, a person's total health can be addressed. Moreover, although chiropractic treatment and craniosacral therapy, performed either separately or together, are not meant to be a cure for individuals with SPD, ASD, ADD, ADHD, or PDD, functional, behavioral, emotional, and educational gains are legitimate goals whenever structure is improved and function follows.

Special acknowledgements to Dr Richard Gelband and Rita Logan.

Charles W. Chapple, DC, FICPA, completed his undergraduate studies at Nazareth College of Rochester, NY, receiving a bachelor degree in biology before earning his doctorate degree in chiropractic medicine from the National College of Chiropractic in 1991. For more information, visit www.drchapple.com.

A Model PLAY Project

Jill Spokojny Guz, OTR;
Robin Crumb, OTR; Karen Goss, OTR

Today, one child in 150 is diagnosed with autism. That's up from one in 10,000 just 14 short years ago. Although the exact cause(s) of the rise in incidence is hotly debated, we know children need help. There is no cure for autism, but early and intensive treatment has proven to be helpful by improving communication and socials skills for children on the autistic spectrum. The National Academy of Sciences recommends that children on the autistic spectrum receive intensive early intervention to achieve the best prognosis. Emerging research strongly suggests that child-centered, relationship-based intervention is very effective in helping young children with autistic spectrum disorders gain language and social skills. Treatment should begin early (18 months to 5 years) and consist of 25 hours per week. A 1:1 or 1:2 ratio of child-to-teacher or child-to–play partner is indicated, using intervention strategies that are engaging and have a strategic direction (eg, social skills or language).

Several interaction-based treatment programs are now available for use with children on the autistic spectrum. Therapists at the Abilities Center, a pediatric therapy facility in Detroit, Mich, have had the opportunity to work directly with Richard Solomon, MD, founder of PLAY Project (Play and Language for Autistic Youngsters). This program, based on Dr Stanley Greenspan's Developmental, Individual-Difference, Relationship-based (DIR) Therapy (also called "Floor-time"), is a newly developed program designed to teach parents to work (play) with their children by using strategies that encourage engagement, language, and social skill development. PLAY Project techniques can be used along with more traditional therapy treatment, such as sensory integration and speech-language therapy.

At the Abilities Center, occupational therapists, physical therapists, speech-language therapists, educational specialists, and support staff have enthusiastically embraced PLAY Project techniques when working with children on the autistic spectrum. Many of the staff of the Abilities Center have been trained directly under the supervision of Dr Solomon. In addition to being the founder of the PLAY Project, Dr Solomon is the medical director of the Ann Arbor Center for Developmental and Behavioral Pediatrics and has been diagnosing and treating children with autism for more than 15 years. He is also a certified faculty member of the Interdisciplinary Council on Developmental and Learning Disorders of DIR.

Abilities Center's PLAY Project consultants have the opportunity to work with parents and their children in the home setting 3 hours per month. The purpose of the home visit is to teach families how to implement the DIR/Floortime strategies. Detailed guidance is provided to ensure that families are capable of engaging their child in stimulating play activities for 15–25 hours per week. Parents are videotaped while "playing" with their child and are offered ongoing feedback to enhance their skills as PLAY partners.

Abilities Center therapists also have the opportunity to work with children at their 8000-square-foot, state-of-the-art facility. Families can choose to bring their children to the center for treatment, which includes an indoor playground, climbing wall, swings, ball pit, moon walk, and a wide assortment of toys and equipment that enhances a child's sensorimotor play options. Parents generally participate in the center-based program 1 hour per week. Parents do the "playing," while the PLAY consultant observes the play techniques used by the parents and then provides encouragement, motivation, and new PLAY techniques. As engagement of the child in play activities increases, perseveration naturally decreases. Engagement starts with sensorimotor play, play is turned into games, and then language is added as the child is able to process this information successfully. Ultimately, the goal is for the child to be able to engage in imaginative play and emotional thinking.

In the summer of 2006, the Abilities Center initiated the PLAY Tutor program. Families use PLAY Tutors to provide the intensive intervention necessary for young children to progress through the levels of functional development as described by Dr Greenspan. This program supported families that were already involved in the PLAY Project program. Parents agreed that the more time their children were engaged in using the principles of Floortime, the better off their children would be. They just didn't have enough hours in the day!

Currently, PLAY Tutors receive training and supervision from PLAY Consultants. Tutors work directly with each child 4-10 hours per week to supplement what their parents are able to provide in the home and in school. The tutors are responsible for choosing age-appropriate activities, setting up the treatment rooms, and directing each session. Sessions are videotaped, and each intern keeps a record of the session. Parents may participate but are not required to,

as they are with the PLAY consultant sessions. The tutor is able to provide one-on-one intensive engagement, which is child centered and begins within the child's comfort zone. The goal is to facilitate the child's progression through the six functional developmental levels as defined by the DIR/Floortime model. Circles of communication are encouraged, while self-stimulating behaviors are naturally decreased.

The therapists at the Abilities Center have found the DIR/PLAY Project model compatible with the treatment approaches already being used with children on the autistic spectrum. An understanding of the child's sensory, motor, and language development helps the therapist identify the child's comfort zone, as well as maintain the child's attention and engagement. The addition of PLAY Project to the Abilities Center has provided a more comprehensive approach to the treatment of children on the autistic spectrum. Young children can now receive a multidisciplinary approach, which includes occupational therapy and/or sensory integration, physical therapy, speech-language therapy, and educational support, which are all focused on progression of the child through the functional developmental levels and directed at the child's inherent potential. Reaching the autistic child's potential requires the involvement of all persons significant in that child's life, including siblings, peers, parents, and school personnel. This approach ensures that families receive the training they need to be successful PLAY partners and are able to incorporate the PLAY principles at home, at school, and in the community.

The PLAY Project has helped professionals at the Abilities Center improve their treatment approach to children on the autistic spectrum. It has become the foundation for all interactions with the children and a parent-training model, which is now used throughout the center. Parents, school personnel, and therapists at the Abilities Center all agree that PLAY Project provides the direction families need to help their children on the autistic spectrum develop the skills to be successful in life.

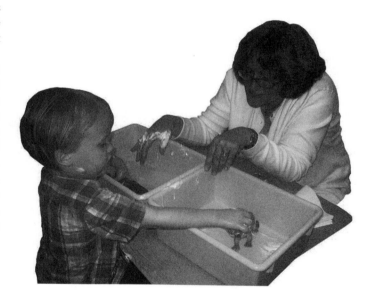

Jill Spokojny Guz, OTR, is president of the Abilities Center, Inc, a multidisciplinary clinic for children with special needs. Robin Crumb, OTR, and Karen Goss, OTR, are occupational therapists at the Abilities Center, which is located in Walled Lake, Mich, near Detroit. Visit their Web site at www.abilitiescenter.com.

Insightful Designs for Home and Clinic Spaces: Bringing Together Occupational Therapy and Creative Design

Elizabeth Meyer-Gross, MSEd, MS, OTR/L

As an in-school, home-care, and private-clinic pediatric occupational therapist for many years, I've had numerous opportunities to provide treatment to children of all ages who have sensory integration dysfunction, or sensory processing disorder (SPD). Invariably, parents are eager to carry out the kinds of therapy at home that they've observed at the sensory gym. In some cases, suggesting to parents that they set up a sensory corner or a "sensory space" has become part of my job when doing home care.

Many parents report that other therapists recommended items to be used as part of a home sensory diet. Actually setting up a space, however, that is therapeutically appropriate for the child, fits the available area, and is aesthetically pleasing within the rest of the home décor, seems a daunting prospect. I'll never forget walking into a small three-room apartment and seeing a ball pit that took up almost the entire living room. The caring mom had purchased it after being told by a therapist that it would be therapeutic for her tactile-defensive son. The son needed a more completely therapeutic but compact space.

That and similar experiences led to my realization that there is a real need for the right kind of assistance. Parents and school administrators could use the help of experienced occupational therapists to analyze the children's individual needs and the available area at the home or school and then, with the help of professional designers, to create, equip, and install a "sensory space." The result would be a space with appropriate sensory-treatment items within the family's or school's budget. It would be aesthetically pleasing, and the choices of materials, colors, sounds, and other elements would reinforce the therapeutic values.

My partner and I operate OT Kids Plus of NY, a placement agency, treatment facility, and sensory gym in Yonkers, New York. When we were planning the "sensory spaces" for our new facility, we called upon a friend, Joan Hannigan, a talented design artist and educational professional, to assist us in the installation of our sensory gym and quiet room, on the basis of our assessment of the needs of the children with whom we work. The final result, through our team's effort, was a beautiful and therapeutic environment.

From the beginning, other professionals and parents who see it have said they would love to have similar spaces. Thus, we formed Sensory Space Design, Inc, to provide consulting, designing, delivering, and installing of wonderful, appropriately equipped places for children to handle their unique sensory interpretations.

An important part of the premise is that all seven senses are at the core of how people understand and relate to those around them, as well as the environment they are in. When one or more of these senses is impaired or fails to be integrated smoothly with the others, an environment can be created by using and manipulating movement, light, colors, sound, touch, and pressure as part of the therapy. It is not simply a matter of gym equipment; the therapeutic value extends to the whole environment.

Our mission and process became clearer as we determined how we could offer our services.

First, a state-certified occupational therapist conducts a complete assessment of the child or children to determine the type of sensory problems to be addressed. In the case of home spaces to be created for individual children, for example, a survey that includes the parents' perceptions and observations of their child's behavior is provided, and the results are analyzed. Is the child an avoider or a seeker of sensory input? Is the child considered to have high arousal or low? Once this assessment is made, the available space in the home, as well as budgetary concerns, are evaluated.

Then the actual planning and design work begins. In consultations with the family or school administrators, a space is designed and equipped to provide sensory items and experiences that offer relief or access to the particular sensations the children fear or crave.

Our designs for sensory spaces in the home are made, first, with the therapeutic needs of the child in mind. In some cases, sensory spaces can be designed to stimulate senses that may be called upon to compensate for the impairment caused by another. Many needs can be addressed, ranging from encouraging adaptive, positive actions (such as increased alertness, better mobility, or initiated movement responses for those with low-level responsiveness to sensory stimuli) to facilitating serenity (such as more modulated or controlled and calm attentiveness needed to learn) for the child who is agitated or anxious and overly stimulated by what he or she senses.

For home installations, we also consider with the family the options for where the space will be located. Ideally, it is a special space dedicated for use by the child with special sensory needs and can be a corner of a child's bedroom, a portion of a family room or basement, or an entire room.

The choices of color, types of music, types of touch and movement devices, lighting levels and methods, tactile experiences, and other sensory elements are specifically determined. Where appropriate, the elements are designed for easy and safe access so that the child can use the area on his or her own. For a child who would benefit from a calming environment, for example, blue might be the predominant color, while bright yellow would be appropriate for a child who needs more alerting. For a child who vacillates from one to the other, half the room can be painted pale blue and the other half bright yellow, and the child can be coaxed to the best area for his mood that day. The room, however, must end up being a place where the child loves to be, and delightful wall murals and other design elements help make it just that.

A sensory room at school or at a clinic is like the smaller sensory space, but it provides a larger therapeutic environment designed to serve children with a wide range of sensory issues. Some children with SPD need a retreat from the tensions, sensory overloads, and anxieties their world can produce. For the child who is visually aroused by everything, this safe-haven can offer comfort in soothing colors, dimmed lighting, and pleasurable, slow-moving visuals, and perhaps provide a dark, quiet tentlike chair or a cushy, enveloping floor pillow. On the other hand, children who crave movement will find release in the rhythm of a pendulum swing or the beat of a small trampoline.

The largest group of individuals who face sensory-integration struggles is people with autism. Their arousal levels can be either high or very high—and a well-designed sensory space can be an important part of therapy. Sensations crash in on them, and they are unable to regulate their reactions and to calm down from the barrage of sights, sounds, or feelings they encounter. The consequences of such a modulation or self-regulation problem are seen in their inability to communicate, their "inappropriate" behaviors that impede learning in traditional settings, and their feeling of being disconnected from peers.

Sensory integration dysfunction or SPD, however, is not restricted to the autistic spectrum. Many children and adults have milder variations of SPD that can interfere with a sense of calm and control. Children with attention-deficit/hyperactivity disorder, or ADHD, have low sensory-arousal levels. They are, as a result, constantly seeking new and different information and sensations—hence the "hyperactivity." A properly designed sensory space can help them stabilize.

Finally, large numbers of children cope quietly with mild forms of SPD but function in the mainstream and grow up to have successful jobs. They, too, would benefit from the advantages of well-designed, aesthetically pleasing sensory spaces.

Elizabeth Meyer-Gross, MSEd, MS, OTR/L, founded Sensory Space Design, Inc, in collaboration with Heather Meyer, OT, and Joan Hannigan, an art professional, to help parents and special-school administrators set up therapeutic sensory spaces. Elizabeth and Heather also work for OT Kids and OT Plus of New York: OT, PT, and Speech Services, PLLC.

Therapeutic Listening: Listening with the Whole Body

Sheila M. Frick, OTR; Sally R. Young, PhD; Gail E. Huecker, MS, OTR/L

Although most of us rarely think about the auditory environment in the course of daily life, children with auditory defensiveness do. They are painfully aware of the way that everyday sounds can feel like an assault from the environment. The experience of these sensitive children provides a window into the powerful effects sound can have—both physiologically and behaviorally—on the human system. Today, there is ever-growing scientific literature on how sound affects us—from the healing effects of music to the deleterious effects of low-level noise.

Good listening skills are necessary for all the activities and relationships of daily life. Today, many children have sound sensitivity in varying degrees, with auditory defensiveness as the extreme. Auditory defensiveness involves an overreaction to certain sounds. Behavioral responses to the offending sounds can include changing levels of arousal—from withdrawal to hyperactivity—as well as extreme emotional responses (tantrums, fighting, hitting, screaming, silliness, etc). Over time, continued exposure to sounds or acoustic environments that are interpreted as threatening or stressful can have a profound effect on a wide variety of behavioral styles and coping mechanisms, including ritualistic behavior and inflexible or controlling behavior.

What Is Therapeutic Listening?

Therapeutic Listening is an individualized auditory program that is embedded within a sensory integrative framework. A Therapeutic Listening program consists of using high-quality headphones and listening to electronically altered music and nature sounds on CDs. There are two 30-minute listening sessions per day. While listening, children are encouraged to participate in a wide range of therapeutic activities. As with most therapeutic regimens, consistency is important for maximum effectiveness. Once a routine is established, most parents and teachers find that implementing the program is not difficult. Initially, a child might be resistant to using the headphones because they are unfamiliar. Once accustomed to them and to the process as a whole, however, a child commonly looks forward to the listening sessions, sometimes even requesting the headphones.

Before birth, the fetus can be observed moving in response to sound. Therapeutic Listening, with its developmental approach, capitalizes on this cause and effect by including individualized proprioceptive-vestibular activities to accompany the listening sessions. These activities can be done easily at home or in school and do not require special equipment. They generally take 10–20 minutes per day and are aimed at regulating the breath and developing and strengthening the core postural muscles and the basic movement patterns of the orienting response.

The music on Therapeutic Listening CDs has been electronically altered to emphasize the parts of the sound spectrum that naturally trigger our attention and elicit the orienting response. As a result, Therapeutic Listening CDs provide the listener with repeated opportunities to orient. As part of the neurological survival system, the orienting response captures attention and modulates sensation.

Sound is processed in all areas of the brain, including the emotional centers deep in the core of the brain. This is one reason that Therapeutic Listening can be so effective. Some children, however, can have strong emotional and/or behavioral responses while using the program. Accessing and expressing the full range of emotion (including negative emotions) is an important part of every child's development.[1] Sometimes expressing strong emotions can make parents or teachers uncomfortable. An experienced clinician will be able to manage these instances through education and explanation or, when necessary, by changing the music protocol. Vital Links, at (608) 222-7436, also offers free phone consultation for trained practitioners who have questions about a specific case.

Therapeutic Listening is a home- or school-based program and usually lasts about 6 months. Consultation in the clinic with the treating therapist can be done on a weekly, monthly, or bimonthly basis, depending on several factors, including the nature of the concerns, the individual needs of the client, and the ability of the parent, teacher, or caregiver to observe and report the child's responses to each CD. Although Therapeutic Listening is not directly covered by insurance, some school districts provide it as part of an overall educational plan, and it can be built into any ongoing sensory integration program for no additional charge. The specialized headphones cost about $140; some clinics arrange for parents to rent the equipment for a small rental fee.

Movement is our natural response to sound. By providing precise, high-quality auditory input in conjunction with proprioceptive-vestibular activities, Therapeutic Listening can have a positive effect on sensory function, the postural muscles and breath, and the nervous system as a whole. As listening skills improve, not only is an individual better able to negotiate interaction with others through an enhanced ability to hear and understand speech sounds, but he or she is also better able to regulate physiological state and to orient and attend to salient sensory information. Having a solid foundation in these important skills supports connection, engagement, communication, and new learning.

Clinical Investigations on Therapeutic Listening

In Vital Links' 2005 opinion survey, all clinicians trained in and practicing Therapeutic Listening were seeing a widespread improvement in issues related to self-regulation and sensory modulation. In fact, over 70% of respondents who had taken the advanced training (N = 246 total respondents) reported improvement in more than half of their Therapeutic Listening cases in the following six categories:

Attention and focus

Energy level

Transitions

Mood

Sound sensitivity

Sensory defensiveness

Hall and Case-Smith echoed these findings in their study of 10 children with SPD.[2] They found substantial improvements in the mean scores on 10 of the 14 subtests on the Sensory Profile. In addition, qualitative data from parent interviews in this study showed widespread improvements in sound sensitivity, energy level, tantrums, eye contact, attention, transitions, and incontinence.

In addition to changes in basic physiological processes, practitioners in our opinion survey reported that Therapeutic Listening can speed up the *rate of client improvement.* In fact, over 87% of all 1053 respondents reported that Therapeutic Listening did speed up the rate of improvement in more than half of their cases. In addition, a full 95% of respondents who had taken the advanced training reported increased rate of improvement in over half of their cases. Optimal cortical function rests on a strong physiological foundation,[3] which, in turn, can speed progress in the higher-level functional skills.

Taking the composite evidence from Vital Links' 2005 survey, Hall and Case-Smith's study,[2] and numerous anecdotal reports from clinicians all over the world, it appears that Therapeutic Listening can potentially affect many of the basic physiological processes that underlie behavior and learning. We are finding that by providing precise, high-quality auditory input along with activities that elicit an adaptive motor response, Therapeutic Listening can go to the root of many sensory processing issues. In fact, Ayres addressed the importance of sound in overall sensory processing by saying that it is a primal form of sensory integration.

A Primal Form of Sensory Integration

The auditory system is closely related to the vestibular system, and both play an important role in integrating sensory information. The auditory receptors have developed out of primitive vestibular mechanisms, and the two systems are linked by their close physical proximity and shared anatomical structures. Neurologically, the two systems have many shared pathways and several common points of integration.[3]

While input from the vestibular, tactile, and proprioceptive systems has traditionally played the major role in sensory integration interventions, we believe that sound has a unique and important role to play, too. Seeing children who do not filter sound well as a result of sensory processing difficulties[3] or who are known to react negatively to sound is common.

Both the vestibular and auditory systems are important to survival, and Ayres maintained that survival-related functions play a particularly important role in sensory integration.[3] Our ears can warn us of danger—even danger that is outside our visual field, and even at night, when we cannot see. Although in modern life we rarely use auditory monitoring to protect us from lions or tigers, the richly endowed survival-based neural networks remain, and we use them to monitor traffic when we want to cross the street or when there are footsteps following us in a dark alley.

In addition, our listening skills serve as a cornerstone in many vocational, academic, and social endeavors.

What Is Listening?

Listening is a whole-brain, whole-body experience. We might think of listening as a process that occurs primarily in the ears; however, in reality, when we listen, the whole brain lights up. Processing sound creates connections in multiple locations in the brain, including the brain stem, the cerebellum, the reticular formation, and the cortex. Since listening involves so many levels in the brain, it exerts influence over a wide range of biological functions, including emotional tone, arousal level, activation of the core postural muscles, and sensory modulation and integration.

Although we may not be aware of it, we listen on both a conscious and an unconscious level. Unconsciously, we continuously monitor the ambient environment, scanning for sounds that may warrant a shift in our attention. When a salient sound does grab our attention, we perceptually "pull" it into the foreground. As a sound comes into the foreground, the orienting response is elicited, and the whole body becomes enlivened and activated.

The Orienting Response

While the orienting response can be elicited by any of the senses, sound is a particularly effective trigger. We are neurologically wired for survival, so when we hear a novel sound, we are compelled to try to answer the question, "What is it?" With this, the orienting response is set in motion—the postural muscles, working in concert with the vestibular system, activate the trunk to position the eyes and ears so they are facing the sound source to gather more information. In this way, listening is an active sensorimotor process that involves the *whole* body.

The orienting response provides behavioral clues to the overall functioning of the autonomic nervous system. As the body becomes set up to investigate and attend to the stimulus, all systems are primed to help achieve that goal. Arousal level is adjusted in response to environmental demand, incoming sensory information is modulated so that relevant stimuli can be processed, eyes and ears seek out the stimulus, and posture is ignited and prepared for action. Because it has such a powerful effect on the whole nervous system, eliciting the orienting response, in and of itself, can have a therapeutic effect. In fact, the orienting response has been equated with sensory modulation because a person cannot orient without the ability to regulate state and to modulate sensory input.

Difficulties with the orienting response and sensory modulation are seen in a variety of diagnostic categories, including autism spectrum disorder, cerebral palsy, attentional difficulties (such as attention-deficit disorder, or ADD; and attention-deficit/hyperactivity disorder, or ADHD), Fragile X, and Down syndrome. When the basic orienting, regulatory, and modulation processes do not function well, attention, behavior, and all higher-level social and academic skills are at risk for developmental delay.

What Is the Sensory Integration and Praxis Test (SIPT)?

The Sensory Integration and Praxis Test (SIPT), developed by A. Jean Ayres, PhD, measures the sensory integration processes that underlie learning and behavior. It is one of the most reliable and standardized assessment tools used by occupational therapists. It consists of a battery of

17 individually administered tests that are used to assess sensory integration difficulties in four domains. These include:

- Form and space, and visual-motor skills
- Tactile discrimination
- Praxis
- Vestibular and proprioceptive processing

The SIPT was designed for children with mild to moderate learning or motor difficulties between the ages of 4 years and 8 years 11 months. Originally designed for the detection and description of symptoms, this tool may also be sensitive enough to measure change from sensory integration interventions. The SIPT battery is not intended to be a comprehensive test and should always be used in conjunction with clinical observation, case history and diagnostic reports, and other pertinent information. Interpretation of the SIPT requires specific professional training.

My World Comes Alive: Sara's Story

Sara was born in Russia and placed in an orphanage at age 2. She remained there until age 4½, when she was adopted by a family in Florida. She spoke no English when she arrived from Russia and began kindergarten. Because of developmental and academic delays, Sara's teachers suggested that she repeat kindergarten. During her second year of kindergarten, Sara was referred for an occupational therapy evaluation, with primary parental concerns being poor safety awareness and lack of impulse control.

Results from the initial parent interview and clinical observations indicated that Sara had increased activity level, poor body awareness, difficulty regulating sleep patterns, postural insecurity to movement, and difficulty with interpersonal interaction. Sara also demonstrated overreactivity to light touch (ie, did not like to be hugged or to give hugs), noise (ie, vacuum cleaners), bright lights, and environmental smells (ie, cooking smells). She chewed on her clothing frequently, demonstrated an attention span of approximately 5 minutes on a sit-down task, and appeared anxious and impulsive.

In addition, Sara demonstrated modulation deficits, particularly with vocal tones, as she spoke in a high, shrill, loud voice. Her respiration patterns were short and shallow, and eye contact was minimal. She was further described as a daredevil and had poor safety awareness. All these behaviors were of primary concern, in addition to the fact that Sara could be "too invasive" socially and that she demonstrated no stranger anxiety. She also appeared easily frustrated, was prone to tantrums, and had difficulty with transitions.

In the clinic, she showed poor trunk strength and control and quickly fatigued in sitting and standing, often slumping at her desk or leaning against things when standing. Sara would move quickly through all motor activities to compensate for slow sustained control. She had difficulty sitting upright at a desk for longer than a few minutes at a time, and spatial and organizational skills appeared decreased.

Sara was only able to attend therapy 1 hour every other week for 60-minute sessions—a total of 15 direct treatment sessions over a 7-month period. In addition to Therapeutic Listening, a sensory diet of home program activities—including the TheraPressure Program;[4] the book, *How*

Letter improvement related to Sara's Story after completing Therapeutic Listening.

Number improvement related to Sara's Story after completing Therapeutic Listening.

Does Your Engine Run?, which outlines the Alert Program for self-regulation by Schellenberger and Williams;[5] and a core postural control and muscular coordination program.

After a few weeks of Therapeutic Listening, Sara's behavior took some dramatic turns. Although she had never been comfortable with touching or hugging, she spontaneously crawled up into her mother's lap and snuggled until she fell asleep. She also began initiating hugs with her grandmother, speaking in a lower voice, and noticing sounds for the first time.

Sara's occupational therapist relays the mother's report,

> One day she was running through the house and she stopped "dead in her tracks" (stopping wasn't something Sara did very often, because she frequently had a "high-running engine" and was often "on the go"). After stopping, she said "Listen Mommy, do you hear those birds chirping?" and she went to the window to look outside. She had never before tuned in to environmental sounds like that.

Her therapist goes on to say,

> *I personally get goose bumps as I think about how neat that was for a little girl who came from a foreign country knowing no English, and how unfamiliar her environment must have been. Sara's drawing with the butterflies and the trees and flowers makes me think of her looking out the window at those birds—this is how her world had opened up and come alive and she began seeing, hearing, and delighting in her surroundings.*

By the 10th week of listening, Sara's teachers reported "her best 2 weeks of school ever," with improved attention span and improved visual spatial skills (see changes in writing letters and numbers). In the final week of therapy, her caregivers reported increased relaxation and more periods of a "quiet-alert state," improved eating patterns, and the capability to put herself to sleep at night.

Sara's before-and-after standardized test results confirmed some of the positive changes that Sara's mother and therapist had been observing in 7 months of treatment. Sensory Integration and Praxis Test, or SIPT, scores changed dramatically (see Figure), as did four subscales on the sensory profile. At initial testing in August, Sara had a Definite Difference in Sensory Seeking and a Probable Difference in Emotional Reactivity, Oral Sensitivity, and Inattention/Distraction. By March of the following year, she had a score of Typical Performance in all categories. Likewise, Sara's pretreatment Quick Neurological Screening Test, or QNST, score was 57, which put her in the "High" category for soft neurological processing deficits. Her posttreatment score was 26, which is only one point away from the category considered "Normal."

As Sara's case demonstrates, the auditory channel can be an important avenue for providing high-quality sensory input when sensory modulation and self-regulatory processes are disordered. Therapeutic Listening, used in conjunction with posture and breath activities that provide

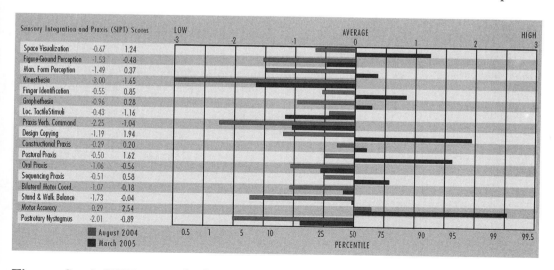

Figure. Sara's SIPT scores, before and after completing the Therapeutic Listening program.

precise vestibular and proprioceptive input, along with other sensory integration techniques, can have an effect on the basic physiology that supports virtually all higher-level adaptive skills. We hope that sound-based interventions will continue to gain acceptance as valuable tools in sensory integrative treatment programs.

References

1. Greenspan SI. *The Growth of the Mind and the Endangered Origins of Intelligence*. Reading, MA: Addison-Wesley; 1997.

2. Hall L, Case-Smith J. The effect of sound-based intervention on children with sensory processing disorders and visual-motor delays. *Am J Occup Ther.* 2007;61(2):209–215.

3. Ayres AJ. *Sensory Integration and Learning Disorders*. Los Angeles, CA: Western Psychological Services; 1972.

4. Wilbarger PL, Wilbarger JL. *Sensory Defensiveness: A Comprehensive Treatment Approach*. Panorama City, CA: Avanti Educational Programs; 2006.

5. Shellenberger S, Williams MS. *How Does Your Engine Run? The Alert Program for Self-Regulation*. Albuquerque, NM: TherapyWorks, Inc; 1996.

Sheila M. Frick, OTR, is the founder of Vital Links, an American Occupational Therapy Association–approved provider of continuing education opportunities that incorporates Therapeutic Listening, vestibular habilitation, and core development. The primary objective of all Vital Links courses is to provide innovative clinical tools and strategies that can be immediately implemented upon course completion in schools, clinics, and homes. Visit www.vitallinks.net for more information.

Sally R. Young, PhD, is the director of research and program development at Vital Links in Madison, Wis. She has worked with adults with severe sensory processing difficulties for more than 25 years in a variety of roles, including teaching expressive arts and adaptive physical education.

Gail E. Huecker, MS, OTR/L, became an occupational therapist in 1992 and has been involved in research studies on sensory integration through Temple University, including a current study on the effectiveness of sensory integration treatment. Gail is the owner of OT 4 Kids, Inc, a private practice in Crystal River, Fla, where she currently practices part-time as an occupational therapist. Her full-time job is mothering her four young children.

A Look at Rhythmic Entrainment Intervention by Its Creator

Jeff Strong

Auditory rhythm has a long history of use for affecting neurological function, with the earliest uses being documented tens of thousands of years ago. These original techniques are some of the most pervasive therapeutic practices known to man, existing on every continent, even among people who had no contact with one another.

As an ethnomusicologist, I was fascinated by the commonality in the techniques within such disparate cultures. I spent over a decade trying to understand how the same basic therapeutic approaches developed when so many other aspects of these societies were vastly different.

The answer, it appeared, was that the physiological mechanisms at work are so powerful that experimentation by each culture resulted in a common finding: You can affect consciousness, cognition, and behavior by using only two specific rhythmic techniques. One consists of a repetitive pulse, while the other involves complex rhythmic structures.

Discovering such commonality among traditional therapeutic rhythm practices prompted another, perhaps more important, question: Can these therapeutic effects sustain themselves outside of the cultural context in which they developed? I believed so, but many of my colleagues did not, believing instead that the rhythm was secondary to the rituals they were imbedded in (and is often attributed to the placebo effect). This led to an odyssey that began in 1992 and has continued to this day, culminating in the development of Rhythmic Entrainment Intervention (REI).

REI is a music-medicine therapy that stimulates and synchronizes the listener's brain. REI is available as some generalized CDs (*Calming Rhythms* and *Focusing Rhythms*) and the REI Custom Program. This is a custom-made, 10-week program that optimizes neurological function.

Auditory Rhythm to Stimulate the Brain

REI is unique in several ways. First, REI uses auditory rhythm to directly stimulate the listener's brain. Other auditory programs use modulated frequency,[1] binaural beats,[2] or simply classical-based music.[3]

Auditory Driving

As I developed REI, my first step was to identify the core mechanisms of the traditional techniques. It turns out that these mechanisms are simple, powerful, and easily understood. First, human consciousness can be directly affected by an auditory stimulus. This is called "auditory driving." Auditory driving states that a listener's brain wave activity will synchronize with the pulsation of an auditory rhythm (provided certain conditions are met).

Traditional practitioners would use a 4-beat-per-second rhythm, which would in turn facilitate a corresponding 4-beat-per-second pulsation in the listener's brain, resulting in bilateral neurological synchronization and a shift in consciousness to a theta state (this is a meditative state). With REI, we double the tempo to synchronize a listener's brain into a relaxed neurological state called *alpha*. This is the state of consciousness where sensory processing is optimized.

Complex Rhythms

The second core mechanism involved in traditional therapeutic rhythm techniques consists of using complex rhythms to activate the brain. Here, complex auditory rhythms stimulate the reticular activating system, a part of the brain that controls sensory input. Applying rhythm—especially complex rhythm—to activate the brain is one level of the stimulation provided by REI. As we conducted research, we discovered another dimension to the rhythms: one that appears to be more important than just complexity. It seems that each rhythm produces a different response.

Once the core mechanisms were discovered, the next step was to determine the best way to deliver the correct stimulus to aid in the areas in which I was interested. Traditional practitioners performed the rhythms live for each person and adjusted their rhythms on the basis of the responses they saw in their patient.

Daily Listening for Long-Term Change

This is where I started—the first 1000 people that REI was used for experienced this one-on-one, live stimulus. They also listened to a recording of one of their live sessions daily in their homes. Daily listening was a departure from tradition, but I felt that people needed the stimulation repeated consistently for a length of time for any long-term change to be expected.

One of the first children that I worked with in this manner was a 7-year-old girl on the autism spectrum. In this case, the girl, let's call her Stephanie, was referred to me because of extreme anxiety. This anxiety affected every aspect of her life: She wasn't able to sleep in her own room and needed to be in constant contact with her mother, and transitions and even minor changes in her environment were a point of crisis for her throughout the day.

She also had marked language and social delays. Her language consisted largely of repeating rote words and phrases. Although she had a large vocabulary, she was unable to communicate beyond her basic needs and desires. Socially, she lacked eye contact and wasn't able to interact appropriately with her peers.

She calmed down within minutes during the first live session, and after the second session she remained calm and was able to sleep in her own room from that night on. Stephanie listened to a recording of her third live session every day for 8 weeks. At 7 weeks, she spontaneously described events in proper sequence for the first time. She was also developing social connections and had begun making friends.

She was mainstreamed at school (she was in a classroom with nonautistic children and had a one-on-one aide), and at 10 weeks, the school psychologist evaluated Stephanie in her classroom and noted that she was "indistinguishable from the 'normal' children in the class." She continued listening to her recording for several more months and eventually no longer required her one-on-one aide.

Universal Calming Effects

This, and many other cases studies, led to a formal study conducted in a public school setting. This study consisted of 16 children aged 6 to 12 who were on the autism spectrum. The results of this study showed almost universal calming effects (only one child was not calm most of the time, and this child ended up not being on the autism spectrum).

Long-term change was clinically significant for anyone who heard the recording at least four times per week. This study caught the attention of several prominent autism professionals and led to a paper written about this study being presented at several professional research conferences (including one organized by The Center for the Study of Autism, led by Dr Stephen Edelson, who went on to design all of our double-blind, placebo-controlled studies).

At this point, my interest in exploring the therapeutic application of auditory rhythmic stimulation techniques deepened. I formed the REI Institute with Beth Kaplan, with no intention of creating a "therapy" that would be available outside of a research environment. Our goal was simply to try to understand how auditory rhythmic stimulation could be used to enhance neurological function.

Over the next 10 years, the REI Institute conducted numerous studies and presented dozens of scientific papers on what we were learning. Two of the key discoveries of this period were that synchronization was universal when certain techniques were applied and that each rhythm used elicited a definite, observable response over time.

Specific Rhythms' Observable Effects

In other words, we found that we could introduce specific rhythms to have a predetermined effect on each listener. To date, we have documented more than 600 rhythms that seem to correspond to symptoms and combinations of symptoms. As a result, we found it was critical to use just the right rhythms for each person to elicit the greatest positive benefits for that person.

During the 1990s, the REI Institute conducted a series of double-blind, placebo-controlled studies to try to understand the best approaches to take in balancing auditory stimulation and synchronization. What we learned, in a nutshell, was that the custom-made CDs are more effective than CDs created for a broad user base.

Custom-made, Revisable CDs

This leads to the second unique aspect of REI: The REI Custom Program is custom-created for each person on the basis of his unique characteristics. By custom-making each CD, we can ensure that the correct level of stimulation is used for that person. In the event that we aren't seeing the results we've come to expect, we also revise the CDs until we see the results we are looking for. The practice of revising the custom-made CDs is the third unique aspect of REI.

Because the REI Custom Program is created for each person, we are able to focus the CDs on the three or four main issues someone faces. As a result, everyone responds differently to his CDs, but we see the most substantial benefits in some general categories. These include anxiety, sleep, self-stimulatory behaviors, language skills, sensory sensitivities and defensiveness, socialization, attention and focus, and aggressive or oppositional behaviors.

Another example of the results with the REI Custom Program (and one most relevant to this article) can be seen with a 10-year-old boy with severe sensory issues. Gerald, as I'll refer to him, saw substantial improvement within just a few days. Before he began the REI Custom Program, he refused to wear shoes or socks, covered his ears whenever music was played, couldn't tolerate headphones, and socially isolated himself from others, often retreating to a dark, quiet room.

Within the first week of listening to his CDs, Gerald was more tolerant of everyday sounds. He also spontaneously joined his extended family outside and began interacting with them. By the second week, he was interacting with his siblings and cousins much more frequently, and by week 4, according to his REI Provider, "He is wearing socks and tennis shoes every day. He now not only allows mom to listen to music in the car, but he often goes to his room and 'rocks out' to his own pop music. He has been more interactive and engaged in activities, as well as initiating appropriate play with other children." He was also able to tolerate headphones for the first time.

Open-Air Environment

This leads to the fourth thing that distinguishes REI from other auditory programs: REI is designed to be used in an open-air environment. That is, we don't use headphones for the implementation of the therapy. The CDs simply need to play quietly in the background once a day (with the exception of the third week, where the CDs are used twice a day). Having the stimulus in the background while the rest of the sensory input of life goes on forces the brain's reticular activating system to work hard to decipher the pattern in the stimulus, while also ensuring that the listener doesn't become overstimulated by the rhythms.

In 2004, we began offering the REI Custom Program through trained providers—we now have hundreds across the U.S. This represented a monumental shift after 22 years of research— research that simply started from my desire to understand why traditional therapeutic rhythm practices were so prevalent around the world.

In spite of our growth and the expansion of REI beyond just research, I am still personally involved in the creation of all the REI Custom Program CDs that leave our office, and am still impassioned by learning more about how auditory rhythmic stimulation can affect individuals with neurological issues.

References

1. Tomatis A. *The Conscious Ear: My Life of Transformation Through Listening.* Barrytown, NY: Station Hill Press; 1992.

2. Oster G. Auditory beats in the brain. *Sci Am.* 1973;229:94–102.

3. Rauscher FH, Shaw GL, Ky KN. Music and spatial task performance. *Nature.* 1993; 365:611.

4. Strong, J. Rhythmic Entrainment Intervention (REI) as applied to childhood autism. Paper presented at: VI International Music Medicine Symposium; October 1996.

Jeff Strong is the creator of Rhythmic Entrainment Intervention (REI) and the founder and director of the REI Institute. He is also the best-selling author of eight books, including AD/HD for Dummies (Wiley, 2004). For more information (and a free DVD) about REI, the REI Custom Program, and our provider training programs, call (800) 659-6644 or visit www.REIinstitute.com.

The S.N.O.T. Protocol: Teaching the Social Rules of Removal and Disposal of Boogers

Rondalyn V. Whitney, MOT, OTR/L, SWC

As an occupational therapist who works with children, I have needed to develop some interesting "protocols," such as how to not stick your middle finger up, how to write your homework without touching the "itchy" part of a pencil or hearing the lead squeak across the page, and respectful gum chewing practice for classroom citizenship. I have helped many students to develop a gag reflex, to classify and tolerate licking of various slimy foods, and to control the muscles that make the "*f*" sound by spitting Cheerios, marshmallows, and other spit-slimed edible projectiles across the room to say "funny" rather than "tunny"! My job is undeniably a blast.

I also work with children to help them pull up their pants after using the toilet, to reach the periarea (the area that toilet paper cleans), to learn about digestion and elimination, and to come to terms with the reality that, indeed, everybody poops. I've concretized the social rules of "butt burps" (we always say "Excuse me" when we invade another's space, even with smells). Perhaps the most popular and in-demand protocol I have developed is how to not pick and/or eat one's own boogers.

The practice of occupational therapy is a blend of theory and practice. The theory I use to support my practice in pediatrics is a blend of psychosocial theories and sensory integration. Odd as it may sound, I have a protocol for each of Freud's stages of psychosexual development and the corresponding *erogenous zone* on the body (oral, anal, phallic, and genital).

When Freud developed his theories in the early 20th century, he was mainly concerned with sexual desire and the occurrences in the early developmental years related to the instincts and appetites germane to sexual urges concentrated in the biological centers of the oral, anal, phallic, and genital areas. Freud felt that the pleasurable sensations and seeking behaviors associated with these biological areas were normal, and that the exploration, fulfillment, and satisfaction of each area allowed the individual to move fluidly on to the next stage of maturity. He was less interested in the "latency" phase, the period of time when a child's development is "on pause." I think this theory aligns with sensory integration theory if you consider that sensory-based practices emerged from the philosophy that we act in ways that help us to organize our senses.

For example, when a child sucks her thumb or has potty problems or rubs her genitals when she is overly challenged by her schoolwork, occupational therapists and/or sensory integration professionals consider the sensory-seeking behavior to be a road map into understanding the neurobiological system. When it comes to boogers, I had to ask myself, "What are the intrinsically motivating factors for nose picking?" and "What are the social and/or developmental aspects of nose picking?" Are the kids who are "digging for gold" redirecting repressed *sexual* desires, or are they providing sensory input to a highly innervated (rich with nerves) area?

As I reflected on this theoretical link between occupational therapy, sensory integration, and Freudian theory, I sorted through my weekly treatments and found that I didn't have a place in Freud's hierarchy for the "booger" protocol. I have the oral phase covered with spitting, slurping with straws, and licking. I have the anal phase addressed with protocols that help students learn to hold on and let go, and to tolerate wiping and Play-Doh (Freud includes play with doughlike, gooey substances as an activity associated with the anal phase). I have a protocol for the phallic stage, when I teach students the socially appropriate rules on self-gratification.

But snot? Boogers? The nose? Where does that fall? I hereby advocate for the inclusion of the *naral* phase of human development. I'm sure Freud would have included it if he had worked more with children!

The nostrils, or *nares*, are interesting holes in your head. In general, we are curious about the holes in our bodies, and, as we mature, we learn more about those holes and how they make us feel if we explore them. Take the first fun hole we learn to play with—our belly buttons. Every parent plays with and tickles a baby's belly button; hey, it's a button! But it is a button with a bottom.

Some holes don't seem as finite, and that's curious…nares, for example, lead straight to the brain to bring sensations of smell immediately to the sensory nerve for olfaction. These two holes are arguably the most socially acceptable holes to stick your fingers into in polite society (everything being relative).

Most people associate the naral zone with smells or olfaction. Olfaction is the only sense that does not pass first through a relay station in the brain, so you can think of it as a nonstop flight, while vision, touch, hearing, taste, proprioception, and vestibular sensations all have layovers at various ports in the head. Now, we can't get a finger into the brain, really, but we can send microscopic beads of scent right back through those one-way channels.

Olfaction is a powerful alerter or calmer to the sensory system. Consider how you feel when you think of the scents of baby powder, roses, baking bread, onions, and your teenage son's gym socks…visceral responses, right? Smells are powerful.

While we think of the nose primarily as a conductor of scent, it has other skills. The nose has loads of tactile and proprioceptive receptors. It feels when we touch it, and it feels more if we touch it inside where it's dark and primitive and secluded. The ancient Greeks thought the infra-nasal depression, the vertical groove under the nose leading to the mouth (the philtrum), was one of the most erogenous spots on the body—and the fingerprint of God.

We can rub the outside of our noses lightly and activate a tactile receptor, and our brain says, "Oh, you touched me." We can gently rub noses with another, like an Eskimo kiss, or we can rub vigorously to prevent an annoying tickle from making us sneeze. When we do that, we activate the proprioceptive sensation (the one in the joints and muscles that makes tickles and wiggles go away). If we *do* rub our nose and there's a booger in there, one with pointy, jagged edges poking our inner sanctuary, we're going to want to go in there and rescue that tender tissue from the invading prickle. Now, I'm a problem solver by nature and by training, and so I set out to solve this problem (mostly as self-preservation during flu season).

Teaching social rules about boogers is not easy. I have polite words to use in each of my protocols and to document in medical charts. For the oral phase of treatments, I can talk about dysphagia and clearing a bolus and tongue thrusts and lateral chews and passive dependence on nonedible chew items for regulating attention. For the anal phase, I can document practices of pericare (caring for the perineum area) and talk about elimination and defecation and stool and bowel movements, and I can work with clients to achieve organization or overcome excessive neatness. If I'm working with treatment protocols targeted to support mature occupational performance in the phallic stage, I produce Cheerios and teach boys to stand at the toilet, take aim, and sink them in the water. We speak in directional terms, such as "erect" and "flaccid," and I can document politely or medically, using words such as genitals, urine, and "self-gratification in densely innervated regions in socially inappropriate manners." Of course, moving on to puberty and beyond, to frigidity and impotence and mutual satisfaction, I'm on fertile ground in today's let-it-all-hang-out media …but naral troubles?

The naral phase, (formerly referred to by Freud as "latent" and so without anything to euphemize) has mucus (snot), nares (nose holes), and the philtrum, but there is no medically euphemized or socially appropriate word for booger. A booger is what it is: a booger. Even Wikipedia has an entry for "booger" and refers to the pearl formed as mucus dries around a particle and hardens, like a formation around an irritant in an oyster (eeeew). So, when referring to partially solidified mucus from the nose, I have to write "booger" on an Individualized Education Plan or a medical chart, or, if speaking to a child, name the offensive object in my grown-up voice and say, *Today we're going to learn about the social rules of boogers.*" When I went on a fascinating quest to understand this unpretentious term, here's what I discovered and share with my clients.

What follows is the protocol I developed. I'm pretty dramatic when I lead it, and I make sure I smear lime Jell-O and peanut butter boogers *everywhere* as I lead the session. We always have a snack after the session: a socially appropriate plate of edible boogers and snot. Freud might say the outcome of this group was the socially appropriate development of the defense mechanism "sublimation," and that this will serve as a tool of socially appropriate behavior in response to the erogenous naral zone related (and here I'm taking a liberty) to the latency phase. I've never had a client eat a booger after attending this treatment session.

Special thanks to Alex who, at age 2, interrupted a lesson plan on "Theories in Occupational Therapy" by saying, "I need a tissue because I had a bless you and all my boogers came out" and inspired this article; and to Stephanie Jordon, OTS, who left sticky-note suggestions and a new box of tissues on my manuscript.

Booger Protocol

Note to teacher/therapist/parent: Start with the colloquial "snot," as you're going to end in a conversation about boogers.

- Snot is human slime or mucus. Mucus is important and is found all over nature. It coats your skin and hair, and when bits of stuff get stuck in your nose hairs, it's the mucus or snot that surrounds it and traps it. When you find a booger, it means your nose is working the way it is supposed to work and keeping the germs out.

- Boogers are dried-up snot or trapped stuff you breathe in, like dust, pollen, germs, sand, fungi, smoke, and germs. Snot traps those invaders and keeps them from getting into your lungs. Boogers are the only word in medicine that doesn't have a "nice" alternative or euphemism to use. For example, instead of snot, the polite term is mucus, but a booger is a booger.
- What is the problem with snot and boogers?

To others, snot and boogers are a problem because:

1. Snot drips out of your nose and gets on other people's stuff or on your hands and arms, which touch other people's stuff.
2. Boogers are germ balls usually covered with snot, and they get on other people's stuff or your hands, and your hands touch other people's stuff.

(This is where I start playing with the peanut butter boogers and Jell-O, making sure to get it all over as much stuff as I can.)

To you, snot and boogers are a problem because:

1. Snot drips out of your nose and gets on your stuff. More importantly, it's uncomfortable in your nose and can be very distracting. It can drip into your mouth, and it tastes salty or yucky and can tickle.
2. Boogers are germ balls. Your body has worked very hard to trap the germs and dirt in a protective cover (your snot) that is full of germ killers while it's in your body. Once you pull a booger out, you have the problem of where to put it.
3. Boogers can hurt. They're sharp and can poke the inside of your nose, and you usually want them to come out.
4. Where you put those boogers matters because they have a tendency to show up again if you smear them on a desk, and they stick to your shirt sleeve or your papers, and then you have your germs back—or worse, someone else's germs.
5. If you eat your boogers, you're eating all those germs and dirt that your body worked hard to get rid of, and you *know* what germs do in your tummy! Diarrhea, throw-up, headaches…

So, there seem to be two *real* problems and solutions:

Problem 1. Even if sticking your finger in your nose feels good, it comes out covered with snot or boogers that are germy and messy.

Solution: *You can rub your nose from the outside, and that gives the same "input" to the tactile system. Or if you have to stick your finger in, you can wrap it in a tissue first.*

Problem 2. You need to do something with the boogers once you get them out.

Solution: *You can use a tissue to wrap the booger in and throw it into the trash can or the toilet. That way, the germs are gone gone gone, just as your body had planned. (Your mouth may be convenient, but it's not a good trash can.)*

S.N.O.T. Lesson

S—Sharing germs
When you sneeze, your body is getting rid of the dirt and germs that are "tickling" the nose. That's why we cover our mouths and noses to keep us from spraying others with our snot and boogers and thereby sharing germs.

N—Nose dirt
Boogers are your body's immune system at work. Snot comes out of the body and wraps a "package" around dirt and germs. Then, you remove them with a sneeze or a cough, or by using a tissue or, sometimes, your finger (eewwww!). Sometimes, people eat their boogers. But your body is trying to *get rid* of that germy nose dirt, so do you really want to eat it???????

O—Others
Other people don't like it when you rub a booger on them or when you pick a booger out of your nose with your hands, because then you touch them or spread your germs in common areas.

T—Tissue
We usually use tissues to catch and capture the germs and then throw them away. A good friend throws the germs in the trash, where they belong.

Remember, good friends keep themselves and their snot and boogers in their own space.

Simple Booger Recipe

3 cups granola, best with raisins or other dried fruit for maximum gross-out factor. (Change the proportions depending on the granola—you want it sticky but dry enough to hold together.)

¼ cup honey or maple syrup

½ cup peanut butter

Mix well with a large spoon or clean hands. Mold into small balls (about ¼ inch). Chill. Serve with spoonfuls of lime Jell-O made with 1½ times the suggested water, so that it does not quite gel and forms a nice, familiar-feeling mucosal bath around the boogers.

Fun sensory additions:
Fruit by the Foot, cut into tiny slivers (red is good, as it looks like blood)
Chopped nuts

Coconut
Chocolate bits
Chopped dates or other dried fruit

Variations:
Use condensed milk instead of honey and add powdered milk.

Use your imagination!

References

1. Netter, F. *Atlas of Human Anatomy*. Summit, NJ: Ciba-Geigy Corp; 1989.

2. Freud, S. *The Basic Writings of Sigmund Freud: Psychopathology of Everyday Life, the Interpretation of Dreams, and Three Contributions to the Theory of Sex*. New York, NY: Random House; 1995.

3. Philtrum. Wikipedia. http://enwikipedia.org/wiki/Philtrum. Accessed November 12, 2007.

Rondalyn V. Whitney, PhD candidate, MOT, OTR/L, is the author of the book Nonverbal Learning Disorder: Understanding and Coping with NLD and Asperger's. She authored the article "A Mother's Occupation: OT for Mothers with Hard-to-Parent Children," which can be found at todayinot.com. Her clinical practice is the Center for Autism and Related Disorders at Kennedy Krieger Institute in Baltimore, Maryland. Research projects include Social Skills Intervention for School-Aged Children (research coordinator) and work on Online Journal Writing for Mothers Parenting Children with Socially Disruptive Conduct (PI). You can find more information about Rondalyn's doings at rondalynwhitney.com and kennedykrieger.org.

The Listening Program: Auditory Stimulation for Improved Social Engagement

G. Alexander Doman

Our ears are always open. Whether busy with the activities that fill our lives in the light of day, or in the midst of a restful sleep under the shadow of night, the auditory sense is feeding our brain information about the environment.

Naturally, we recognize the significant role the auditory system plays in attention, listening, and learning. Its role in balance, posture, and spatial awareness is also implicit.

Many children and adults experience difficulties processing auditory information. Some of these far-ranging challenges include:

Auditory attention

Hypersensitivity to sounds

Filtering out background sounds

Temporal processing

Auditory memory

Understanding the meaning of what is being communicated

As the understanding of the neurobiological mechanisms of auditory function advances, so does our ability to develop and study the effects of auditory stimulation, both on brain organization and as an intervention strategy.

Researchers have identified a link between the middle ear and social engagement that provides insight into why some children may demonstrate atypical behaviors and communication difficulties in certain situations and environments.

Middle Ear and Social Engagement

One clearly explicit model of a link between the middle ear and social engagement is provided by The Polyvagal Theory, formed by Dr Stephen Porges at the University of Illinois at Chicago. He links the evolution of the neural regulation of the heart to affective experience, emotional expression, facial gestures, vocal communication, and social behavior that is responsive to the behavior of others. The theory proposes that the neural control of the heart is neuroanatomically linked to the neural control of the muscles of the face and head through mechanisms of the vagus, or tenth cranial nerve.[1]

The vagus nerve, a primary component of the autonomic nervous system, exits the brain stem and has two branches that regulate the striated muscles of the head and face (eg, facial muscles, eyelids, middle-ear muscles, larynx, pharynx, and muscles of mastication) and several visceral organs, (eg, heart and gut).[2] Porges suggests that specific neural circuits can compromise social engagement in some psychiatric and behavioral disorders, including autism. Social engagement is dependent, in part, on the control of the muscles of the face and neck, which enable us to express a wide range of emotions in ways that others around us can detect, enjoy, and respond to. A key to comfortable social engagement is the vagal nerve innervation of two tiny muscles in the middle ear.

The two muscles of the middle ear are the tensor tympani and the stapedius. Together, they regulate the stiffness of the tympanic membrane (eardrum) and the ossicular chain (consisting of three bones: malleus, incus, and stapes) as a pathway of sound conduction to the inner ear. These muscles must function properly to protect the inner ear from loud sounds and to attenuate low frequencies so that the higher frequencies contained within the human voice can be discriminated. This is especially important with speech in the presence of background noise. Poor speech discrimination with background noise is a common auditory processing problem. This is often coupled with auditory hypersensitivities.

If the middle-ear muscles are not functioning properly, the nervous system can be bombarded with unwanted sound. We have no "ear lids," and thus no protection from this assault. Children who experience auditory sensitivities may be unable to modulate sensations received in the middle ear and may experience the autonomic nervous system state of fight or flight. They may appear hypervigilant. When they can't escape (flight) from seemingly threatening sensory experiences, they may act out defensively (fight). In extreme cases, a child may withdraw and completely shut down. Behaviors such as covering the ears, aggression, rocking, humming, and self-stimulation may be observed. The child may exhibit a lack of facial expression, make poor eye contact, show little interest in others, and have a flat, monotonal voice devoid of rhythm.

Have you ever attempted to carry on a conversation in a noisy, crowded restaurant? Then you will understand that socialization can be very difficult in a challenging sound environment. The noise creates a certain level of nervous tension. It becomes a challenge to modulate the middle-ear muscles to listen and speak, to make eye contact, and to read and display positive facial expressions. This stressful experience may result in agitation and a desire to exit from the situation, causing you to become socially disconnected.

The social engagement system is intimately related to stress reactivity.[2] Sensitivity to the social engagement behavior of others also decreases.

Lower-level needs, including physiological and safety needs, are prioritized before higher-level needs, such as love and belonging, esteem, and self-actualization can be met. If one is merely trying to survive, one cannot express or experience love, belonging, or intimacy, much less be confident, learn, problem solve, and show empathy and acceptance of others. Some of the very qualities that make us distinctively human are impaired.

Intervention

To improve spontaneous social behavior, Dr Porges has proposed that an intervention must stimulate the neural circuits that regulate the muscles of the face and head. Theoretically, once the regulation of these structures is activated, social engagement and communication will spontaneously occur as natural emergent properties of the biological system.[1]

The Listening Program (TLP) method uses music-based auditory stimulation to modulate the regulation of the middle-ear muscles. The theory is that the middle-ear muscles need to be regulated during listening, and the nerves that regulate the muscles are linked to the nerves that regulate the other muscles of the face and head involved in social engagement.[1] TLP is engineered to do this, and included in the method are processes that stimulate and exercise the neural pathways involved in listening and simultaneously stimulate the function of other aspects of the social engagement system.

Technical Details of TLP

Since TLP was introduced in 1999, parents and providers have recurrently reported a reduction in hypersensitivity to sounds, with improved communication and social engagement. When the regulation of the middle-ear muscles improves, so does comfort and safety in the environment. When a listener no longer has to devote his internal resources to comfort and safety, he becomes available to listen, learn, communicate, and engage in prosocial behaviors.

TLP is a patent-pending, music-based auditory stimulation method that is intended to improve auditory, vestibular, and other brain functions. It involves, in part, listening to acoustically modified music through headphones. The listening schedule is 5 days per week, 15–30 minutes per listening session. The program length is typically 5 months and is individualized to meet the needs and goals of each listener. Listening can be done for shorter and longer time periods. In addition, certain programs can be delivered through speakers when a person cannot tolerate headphones. The method is normally integrated within academic and therapeutic programs in the home, at school, and in the clinic.

TLP incorporates the most advanced psychoacoustic processes, including the highest-quality music available, recorded specifically for the method at 24-bit 192-kHz in high definition by using Advanced Brain Technologies' (ABT's) Spatial Surround process delivered with Dolby Headphone technology.

The music consists of classical pieces performed by the award-winning Arcangelos Chamber Ensemble. The compositions are principally by Mozart, with Haydn, Vivaldi, Corelli, and Danzi, offering a rich tapestry of sound with instrumentation of strings and woodwinds.

TLP includes four training categories: full spectrum, sensory integration, speech and language, and high spectrum. This progressive structure allows for refined stimulation and training at any point in the program. To accommodate individual listener preferences, there are options to follow a program with or without sounds of nature. While many prefer to enjoy and focus on the exquisite music, others—especially children—benefit from the novelty of combining music with beautiful sounds from nature.

The program is available on CD and iListen. The CD version includes 10 60-minute albums, an easy-to-use guidebook, a portable CD wallet, listening schedules, and free access to online listener resources.

iListen is an iPod with preloaded music (uncompressed), with the 10 60-minute albums and a library of music from the Sound Health collection (music for relaxation, thinking, etc), as well as the guidebook, carrying case, listening schedules, and free access to online resources.

A recent technological development was the introduction of ABT Bone Conduction Technology. It combines the experience of listening through specialized headphones with subtle vibration to the skin and skeletal system, engaging the whole body and brain in the listening process. This multisensory approach accelerates and expands the benefits of TLP. It can be particularly targeted to listeners with social engagement problems, so that they become more likely to benefit from the program. This portable equipment is compatible with iListen and portable CD players.

TLP is available exclusively through an international network of professionals who receive extensive training, certification, and continuing education through ABT. The providers offer information, assessment, individualized program development, and support to their clients. Parents and professionals may contact ABT for a free consultation or referral to a TLP provider by phoning (801) 622-5676 or by visiting *www.thelisteningprogram.com.*

ABC Modular Design

TLP's patent-pending ABC Modular Design provides appropriate training for social engagement by effectively exercising the auditory system. The training has three phases: "accommodation/warm-up," "training/workout," and "integration/cool-down"—akin to a "sensory diet" for the ears.

Each 60-minute TLP album contains four 15-minute modules. Each module provides three phases of stimulation. The first phase, "A," relaxes the listener, readying her nervous system to benefit from the more intensive stimulation of the "B" phase. This is the phase in which a technology called *audio bursting* stimulates and exercises the neural pathways involved in listening and simultaneously stimulates the function of other aspects of the social engagement system. The listener is then guided to a relaxed state during the final "C" phase.

These modules integrate progressive entrainment processes of tempo, music complexity, and various psychoacoustic processes that regulate arousal levels, providing the greatest opportunity to benefit from the program. As Dr Porges suggests, interventions to improve spontaneous social engagement should ensure that the context elicits in participants a neuroception of safety that allows the social engagement system to function.[1] *Neuroception* is a term coined by Porges to describe how neurocircuits distinguish whether situations or people are safe, dangerous, or life threatening.

A safe, comfortable listening setting with a context of positive association, incorporating the ABC Modular Design within TLP, helps to provide a neuroception of safety for the listener.

Michael

At age 5, Michael was hypersensitive to sound, touch, and multisensory input and was unable to modulate this type of sensory information effectively. During the course of the day, he would quickly reach his sensory limit, responding by exhibiting negative behaviors, withdrawing, or shutting down. At that time, he was attending a private preschool three mornings a week and was receiving limited services, including occupational therapy and speech therapy. Michael was also on a waiting list for a school specializing in autism spectrum disorders. His diagnosis was attention-deficit/hyperactivity disorder, pervasive developmental delay not otherwise specified, and sensory processing disorder.

Michael was involved in a pilot research study on TLP at Primary Children's Medical Center (PCMC) in Utah. The investigator was his occupational therapist, Bryan Gee, OTD, MS, OTR/L. TLP was initially introduced in his occupational therapy sessions and was then followed through by his parents at home.

Intake and pre- and posttesting included a client history, listening checklist, sensory profile, Peabody Developmental Motor Scales 2nd Edition, and video tape. According to the test results, Michael responded to TLP with moderate improvement, which was the criterion required by PCMC to expand the use of TLP to be offered to the local community.

Michael's mother videotaped him as he participated in two school musical programs. In the preprogram video, he demonstrated a rapid decline in social engagement as the school program progressed through several holiday songs. Michael's facial affect flattened, he covered his ears and eyes, rocked himself, and progressively shut down as he became increasingly overloaded by all the activity and bombardment of sound.

Observing Michael in the postprogram video, you see a very different child. He is paying attention, smiling, dancing, has excellent motor timing and coordination, initiates and maintains eye contact, and actively sings throughout a nine-song program, completely engaged with the other students. To the lay observer, it is difficult to differentiate him from his peers.

In the course of his initial TLP program, Michael greatly improved his ability to modulate sensory input, began to engage in imaginary play, had reduced hyperactivity, and expressed appropriate emotions with adults and his peers. According to his speech therapist, his receptive and expressive language skills improved, as did his social skills. Michael now follows multistep directions, maintains good eye contact, and exhibits increased facial expression, reduced sensitivity to sound and touch, and improved emotional regulation.

Consequently, TLP continues to be an integral part of Michael's everyday routine. He was discharged from therapy and is no longer on the waiting list for the specialized school, as he is currently attending and thriving in a regular-education, first-grade class.

References

1. Porges SW. Neuroception: a subconscious system for detecting threats and safety. *Zero Three J*. 2004;May:19–24.

2. Porges SW. The Polyvagal Theory: phylogenic substrates of a social nervous system. *Int J Psychophysiol*. 2001;42:123–146.

3. Doman GA. Unlocking potential: using The Listening Program to help individuals with autism spectrum disorders improve auditory processing. *Autism Asperger's Digest*. 2005;November-December:18–25.

G. Alexander Doman is the founder, president, and CEO of Advanced Brain Technologies (ABT), a neurotechnology company that develops and distributes interactive software and music programs for the improvement of memory, attention, listening, academic skills, sensory processing, brain health, peak performance, and more. Prior to founding ABT, he served as executive director of the National Academy for Child Development. For the past 15 years, his career has been focused on research, product development, and education, primarily in the areas of psychoacoustic music technologies and brain fitness software. He has co-authored two new books for release in 2010–2011, which will be available at advancedbrain.com. He can be reached at alex@advancedbrain.com.

Questions about Michael may be directed to:
Bryan Gee, OTD, MS, OTR/L
Clinical Assistant Professor of Occupational Therapy
Academic Fieldwork Coordinator
Department of Physical and Occupational Therapy
Idaho State University
E-mail: *geebrya@isu.edu*

Visual Support Using SticKids: An Occupational Therapy Model for Using Visuals to Support Those with Sensory Needs

Meryle Lehn, BOT(c)

Many children with sensory difficulties have problems in these areas:

- Language, communication, and making choices
- Memory and attention
- Sequencing and schedule development

A helpful strategy is the use of visuals, historically used in the fields of speech pathology and applied behavioral analysis.

However, parents, teachers, or therapists who support these children may find it overwhelming to explain the complexity of sensory support strategies to others. Delivering these strategies effectively can be even more overwhelming! The use of visuals within the occupational therapy framework to teach and deliver sensory strategies was born out of these challenges.

My use of visuals as an occupational therapist has evolved with the focus on the dynamics between how a visual is used in relation to the child and the occupational task. The manner of using the visuals can be seen in a developmental progression:

- Support for the Adult but Incidental for the Child: During playful therapy time for infants and toddlers, you can use visuals to create planners and prompts that support you, the adult, in organizing a seemingly casual presentation of therapeutic activities. The child may see the pictures but is not expected to attend to them.

- Part of Free Play: While an early preschooler is doing the task, you may casually position a visual card beside or amongst the child's task. Turn the card over after that task is done in celebration of completion, or have the child assist in gathering up the cards afterwards. This is done in a casual, nonstructured way.

- Reflective Approach: For a slightly older preschooler or prekindergartener, use the visual cards to reflect on the child's activities and show them to Mom or Dad to "visually share" the events of the day or session.

- Play and Choose: Once the kindergarten-aged child (or a child with a developmental equivalent) becomes familiar with the visuals, use them during tasks and play. Gradually have the child participate in picking his next task. Then build in games, such as "Your Turn…My Turn" for card and activity selection, or turn a few cards upside down and play a game of "Pick and Flip."

- Plan toward Challenging Events: For the next developmental level, the goal is not to "schedule" a child for the full day, but rather to facilitate therapy sessions and to help a child through tough events. These may include dressing, having a bath, or coping with a world that is too prickly, bright, or loud. Offer the child support strategies before, during, and after challenging events to help her regroup.

- Trackers and Planners: For older children and support caregivers, formal trackers and full-day schedules can help with:

  - Promoting collaboration and follow-through

  - Understanding, choosing, and participating in needed therapy events as the children move toward eventual self-regulation.

A generalized approach will often evolve, once skills and strategies have become entrenched in a child's day. At that point, only an occasional, incidental, or reflective visual planner or prompt may be needed to help maintain the newly gained skills.

The use of visuals does not need to go through a full progression, as outlined above. It will vary according to the needs and preferences of those involved.

The value of visuals in delivering sensory-based occupational therapy led to SticKids!

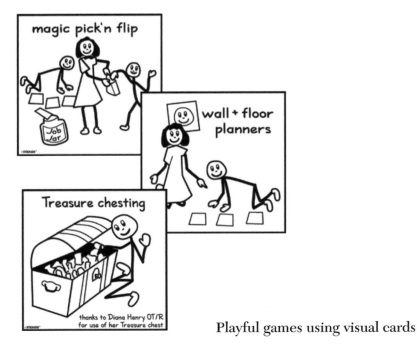

Playful games using visual cards

Planners and Trackers (Weekly Planner, Treasure Chest, Key Ring are pictured)

Making your own visuals can be rewarding. Start with the "sticky" moments in your child's day, and depict them on small cards. Or, if you are not inclined to make your own, try SticKids. SticKids is an interactive software program that uses visuals to create activity cards and planners. It was developed to support children with sensory challenges, ranging from autism to attention deficit to the healthy child with mild sensory and motor needs.

As we know, these children may experience highly tuned or atypical processing of sensory information from external sources of touch, vision, smell, taste, and sound, and from the internal senses of muscle and joints, motion, balance, and touch registration. Atypical processing may appear as:

- Over- or underresponsivity to sensory input
- Excessive seeking or avoiding of sensory input in daily events
- Emotional sensitivity, meltdowns, or need for retreat
- Difficulty with focus, arousal, and self-regulation in everyday tasks
- Reduced quality in motor response (involving coordination, balance, tone, planning, or sequencing), as the motor skill may have been based on misinterpretation of sensory information

The visuals in SticKids are suitable for toddlers to teens and for mildly to severely affected children. They may be used for a single child or for a whole class.

The SticKids visuals are grouped by folders on the computer. Each folder has a category, such as Motion, Pressure 'n Touch, Heavy Work, Suck Chew 'n Breathe, Retreat, and Routines 'n Planning. They are color coded according to likely alerting or calming effects. Here are examples:

Motion

Alert and organize the mind and body.

Pressure 'n Touch

Calm and settle down with a get-ready, regrouping, or transition strategy.

Heavy Work

Alert and calm with motion and deep pressure.

Suck, Chew, 'n Breathe

Organize and alert to help listen and focus.

Retreat

Reduce sensory overload (visual, auditory, and physical).

Routine 'n Planning

Build in cognitive support strategies with familiarity, predictability, and prewarnings.

Two other folders:

Tips, Tools, 'n Doing

Provide strategies for task or tool modification and for activities of everyday "Doing it" events.

Clinic Time (in the Therapist Version)

Promote child participation in selecting, planning, and adapting therapy session activities.

StiCKids has recently introduced a self-regulation program featuring StiCKid, the "Critter meter," and effect icons, "Turtle" and "Bunny." They indicate what the activity will do for the child and are generally color coded according to the activity groupings.

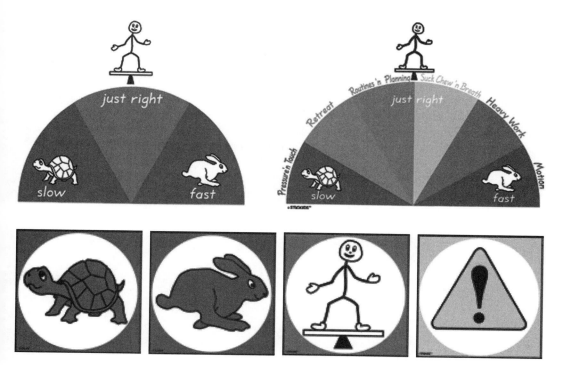

Turtle Speed Indicates the activity may calm the child
Bunny Speed Indicates the activity may increase the child's alert level

Just Right Promotes both calming and alerting outcomes
Caution Is assigned to activities where care must be taken

Mini-icons alongside pictures in the folders on the computer may match mini-icons on various planners and activity cards. (Many activities have several effect icons, as the response can vary, depending on the child and how the activity is presented.)

While using SticKids visual activity cards and planners or any set of visuals, it is very important to:

- Facilitate the child's choice and to enhance the child's dynamic participation—not to impose your own wishes

- Allow for creative adapted play by the child—not to overstructure with planners, visuals, or a regimented exercise routine

- Interact and play with the child—to take his lead and use your visual activities cards in a fun, playful, gamelike manner

Meryle Lehn, OTR, is a Canadian SIPT-certified occupational therapist who has had a special interest in children with sensory challenges since the mid-1970's. SticKids came to fruition thanks to support of family; feedback and guidance from professionals in the field, such as Susanne Smith Roley, PTN, Diana A. Henry, OT, and Lucy Jane Miller, PhD, OTR, FAOTA; the SPD Foundation; and Theresa May-Benson of OTA Watertown, as well as numerous other therapists, parents, teachers, and kids who have given wonderful feedback as the product developed SticKids software to create visuals, therapeutic planners, and wellness strategies for sensory challenges, differences, and regulation can be accessed at www.stickids.com. Meryle Lehn is available for workshops.

PART TWO
General Insights

Position Statement on Terminology Related to Sensory Integration Dysfunction

Lucy Jane Miller, PhD, OTR, FAOTA;
Sharon Cermak, EdD, OTR/L; Shelly Lane, PhD, OTR/L;
Marie Anzalone, ScD, OTR; Jane Koomar, PhD, OTR/L

Introduction

As the field of sensory integration dysfunction has matured and researchers have learned more about this condition, many people have realized that it is time to clarify terminology. Although occupational therapists (OTs) usually understand one another when using the term *sensory integration dysfunction* (sometimes abbreviated DSI), physicians and other health professionals without familiarity with the theory, assessments, and intervention techniques frequently do not share the same knowledge base and may hold a more neurobiological view of the term sensory integration (SI). Since physicians are responsible for the total care of the child—and in many cases provide a referral for OT services, which requires a diagnosis—using a diagnostic term that is more consistent with a physician's perspective seems appropriate. However, due to the wealth of literature related to SI in occupational therapy theory and intervention, the continued use of the term SI when applied to those aspects of SI seems appropriate. This will enable us to retain historical and current published information related to the SI frame of reference within our profession.

We are, therefore, proposing to update the diagnostic terminology used in sensory integration. This article describes a proposed system for sensory integration terminology to differentiate the disorder from both the *theory* and the *intervention* techniques by using occupational therapy with an SI approach. The new nosology proposed for the diagnostic categories included under Dr Ayres' original concepts uses *sensory processing disorder* as a global umbrella term for three primary diagnostic groups and five subgroups of this disorder (see Figure).

In this nosology, *sensory processing disorder* is the umbrella term that encompasses all forms of this disorder, including three major categories (sensory modulation disorder, sensory discrimination disorder, and sensory-based motor disorder) and the subtypes found within each. Detailed descriptions of each of these subtypes will be published separately or can be found at *www.SPDFoundation.net*.

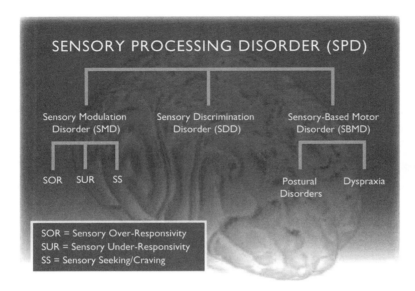

Figure. A new taxonomy for the identification of sensory processing disorders.

Detailed Description

Dr A. Jean Ayres, a researcher and pioneer in this field, coined the term *sensory integration dysfunction*. She used the term throughout her professional career (1954–1988) to describe atypical social, emotional, motor, or functional patterns of behavior that were related to poor processing of sensory stimuli.

Dr Ayres chose the term for two reasons. First, it related to her hypothesized theoretical model, which posited an underlying neurological impairment in the ability to transfer sensory information efficiently between sensory systems in the brain. Second, the term referred to her proposed intervention model, which involved the use of sensory stimuli in one domain to affect performance in another domain (eg, the use of deep pressure, or proprioceptive input, to decrease overresponsivity in the tactile domain). During intervention—occupational therapy using a sensory integration frame of reference—two or more sensory domains are actively used concurrently. Often, action in one or more sensory systems (or provision of one or more sensory stimuli) supports the child as he or she makes an adaptive response to a challenging situation involving another sensory system. An adaptive response occurs when a child engages in activities of increasing difficulty and makes a successful response.

Over the years in practice, the root term, "sensory integration," has been commonly used in four different ways. It is used to refer to:

- A theory (sensory integration theory)
- A diagnosis (based on a sensory integration assessment)
- A functional pattern (normal sensory integration abilities)
- A remediation approach (sensory integration intervention)

Notably, none of these uses corresponds to the neurobiologic meaning of the term *sensory integration*, which refers to a neuronal process that occurs at a cellular level. This can only be observed by using invasive electrophysiologic recording techniques (such as those used in animal research). Sensory integration in this connotation depends on the convergence of excitatory signals from multiple sensory modalities onto (a) a single neuron or (b) networks of neurons. Sites where convergence of sensory input from different sensory modalities occurs are present in many regions of the brain.[1-4]

We selected the term *sensory processing disorder* for two reasons. First, common use in the neurobiology literature indicates deficits in taking in, interpreting, and responding appropriately to sensory input. Second, the lay use of the word "process" refers to a particular method of doing something, generally involving a number of steps or operations that lead to a specific outcome. We propose that the word "process" within the context of "sensory *processing* disorder" captures the series of steps that are disrupted as a result of impairments in sensory detection, modulation, and/or interpretation in children with this dysfunction. In this disorder, atypical behaviors occur in the "process" of discerning a sensory stimulus and making a motor or behavioral response. At this time, we believe that *sensory processing disorder* constitutes a more effective label for facilitating communication between OTs and other professionals.

In summary, we propose that:

- The *theory* is referred to as "sensory integration theory based on the work of Dr A. Jean Ayres."

- The *diagnostic* label is "sensory processing disorder" (SPD).

- The *assessment* terminology includes either the term *integration* or *processing*. As the primary assessment (age 4.5 to 8 years) for sensory processing disorder is the Sensory Integration and Praxis Test (SIPT), use of the term *sensory integration* is logical in that context. Therapists who are certified in SIPT administration would refer to themselves as "certified in sensory integration assessment." However, comprehensive evaluation reports that include tests and supplemental clinical observations of sensory functioning other than the SIPT may be more interpretable by other professionals when findings are related to sensory processing disorder, including sections on symptoms of sensory modulation disorder, sensory discrimination disorder and sensory-based motor disorders, if relevant to the individual child being evaluated.

- The *intervention* label is reserved for therapy that is based on Ayres' original principles and has advanced further as our understanding has evolved to include such elements as a focus on functional performance, participation in natural contexts, and family-centered care. Recommended is that the intervention description include both the discipline and the frame of reference, for example: "OT using principles of sensory integration," or "OT using a sensory integration frame of reference or approach." Only therapists with specific education in this intervention (preferably those with advanced training, including a mentored experience) should use this therapeutic method. Centers or programs specializing in OT using a sensory integration frame of reference will continue to be identified as such.

We propose this change as a way to clarify diagnostic categories for children with sensory symptoms. We are actively engaging with current diagnostic classification system revision committees, advocating for inclusion of this new nosology, in part or in whole, in revised taxono-mies when they are published (eg, *Diagnostic and Statistical Manual of Mental Disorders—V* and *Diagnostic Classification [DC] of Developmental and Mental Health Disorder: 0-3-Revised and DC: 0-3-II*). Formal recognition of this differential diagnosis will stimulate multidisciplinary research into the underlying mechanisms of this poorly understood condition and facilitate the acquisition of services and support for children with this disorder and for their families.

We hope that individuals in the community concerned about sensory integration dysfunction—parents, occupational therapists, physicians, educators, and others—will consider this nosology. We see the transition in this terminology as a process that will continue to evolve as we obtain more empirical data that better define this disorder. Specialists in the field should continue to discuss this issue and grow, adapting new terminology as needed on the basis of research and practice needs.

References

1. Kandel ER, Schwartz JH, Jessell TM, eds. *Principles of Neural Science*. 3rd ed. East Norwalk, CT: Appleton & Lange; 1991.

2. Miller LJ, Lane SJ. Toward a consensus in terminology in sensory integration theory and practice. Part 1. Taxonomy of neurophysiological processes. *Sensory Integration Special Interest Section Q*. 2000;23(1):1–4.

3. Schroeder CE, Lindsley RW, Specht C, Marcovici A, Smiley JF, Javitt DC. Somatosensory input to auditory association cortex in the macaque monkey. *J Neurophysiol*. 2001;85(3): 1322–1327.

4. Wallace MT, Meredith MA, Stein BE. Integration of multiple sensory modalities in cat cortex. *Exp Brain Res*. 1992;91(3):484–488.

Lucy Jane Miller, PhD, OTR, FAOTA, is founder and executive director of STAR Center and the Sensory Processing Disorder Foundation. Contact her at www.spdfoundation.net. Sharon Cermak, EdD, OTR/L, is a professor at Boston University. Shelly Lane, PhD, OTR/L, is a professor at Virginia Commonwealth University. Marie Anzalone, ScD, OTR, is an assistant professor at Columbia University. Jane Koomar, PhD, OTR/L, is the director of OTA-Watertown and president of the Spiral Foundation.

Vision: A Piece of the Puzzle in Sensory Processing Disorders—Part 1

Charles Shidlofsky, OD

Sensory processing disorder (SPD) is a relatively new term that describes a spectrum of signs and symptoms present in some children as a result of poor neural processing. There have been estimates that this group of disorders may be present in up to 25% of the general pediatric population. Visual processing problems are a common component in all sensory processing problems and are quite often missed or misdiagnosed. Approximately 80% of all information entering our sensory system comes through our visual system. The visual system is the only sensory system with a motor component, making it a very complex sensory gathering system.

When I was young, I struggled with school and reading. I had long thought that I had some sort of processing problem or learning problem. It seemed that my system was inefficient, forcing me to study significantly longer than others to grasp the same concepts. Additionally, I was very sensitive to certain materials and seams and tags in my clothes. I also had trouble in large classrooms, with background noise always distracting me.

When I started in practice 17 years ago, I set out to determine how to enhance my visual processing, to resolve at least those problems. I used what I learned in school, plus some experimentation with different optical principles, and ultimately did resolve my visual issues. I had no idea that treating visual processing problems would become the focus of my career.

Early in my career, I started noticing children who had issues similar to mine. After I resolved my own visual issues, I started applying what I learned to help children. I learned a lot from those children and started to understand what caused these problems. I soon recognized that the visual components were not the only piece to this processing problem; they were far more complex than just that. Soon after, I met some speech pathologists and occupational therapists who also knew that they didn't have all the pieces and were searching for a visual answer. Collectively, we realized that sensory processing problems were made up of many interacting pieces of a puzzle. Thus, I started down the path of search and discovery.

Does Perfect Vision = 20/20?

When most people go to the eye doctor, the ultimate goal is getting that person to see 20/20. What does 20/20 mean? Literally, it means that what you see 20 feet away is what a "normal" person can see from 20 feet. From a visual standpoint, it is your identification system or your "What is it?" system. This is the focal system, consisting of cells called *parvo cells* (Figure). This is probably the most important component of your visual system, but not the only component.

I call the other components the visual processing skills. These consist of focusing, eye teaming ability, and eye movement ability. This system answers the question of localization, or "Where is it?" and self perception, or "Where am I?" The "Where" system consists of cells called *magno cells* (Figure).

Anatomy of Vision

The eye has millions of nerve fibers that originate in the retina and terminate in various parts of the brain. At the level of the retina, the parvo pathway originates in the central retina. Because of that, it deals with identification, color contrast, and detail.

The magno pathway originates primarily in the peripheral retina and deals with contrast, movement, and luminance information. Magno cells mediate the ability to attend to things visually. This magno pathway provides a conduit through which visually significant objects can rapidly attract attention and subsequent stimulation of vision. We don't use the magno pathway to see,

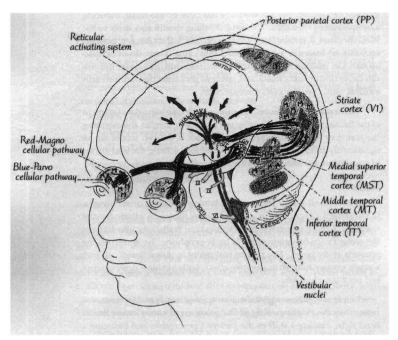

Figure.
Components of the
visual system.

but it is an important component in our process of seeing. Both pathways leave the retina through the optic nerve and cross over to enter the brain.

About 80% of the retinal fibers (primarily from the central retina) terminate in the back of the brain at the visual cortex. This pathway is utilized for both conscious and unconscious visual processing and functions only with the eyes open. The fibers from the central retina provide information about color and detail (identification). Fibers from the peripheral retina also affect this area with information about movement, location, speed, size, and shape. Together, these fibers answer the questions: "What is it?" and "Where is it?"

Approximately 18% of the retinal fibers (primarily from the peripheral retina) travel to the midbrain for unconscious use in spatial awareness. This pathway functions with the eyes open or closed and engages in two-way communication with the auditory, vestibular, and tactile/kines-thetic systems. These fibers answer the question, "Where am I?"

The remaining 2% of fibers travel to the limbic system and other centers that regulate the body and mind functions. This pathway is utilized to trigger emotion.

Visual Attention: A New Basis of Thought

The study of visual attention is one of the hottest areas of study in vision science. For years it has been difficult to study the visual pathways from the eyes to the brain. Now, with the advent of functional magnetic resonance imaging, or fMRI, and positron emission tomography scanning, or PET, we have a better working knowledge of the visual pathways and their interaction with other sensory pathways. We also now know that vision not only occurs in the visual cortex (occipital lobe), but some components of vision also occur in the parietal, temporal, and frontal lobes, as well as the midbrain and cerebellum.

In our first few years of life, we evolve our neuromuscular system from gross motor to fine motor and finally to oculomotor skills. Oculomotor skills should complete the developmental process around age 6. At the same time, our attentive style develops from a movement/touch-based system (in infancy) to an auditory-based system and then ultimately to a visual-based attentive system. Both the neuromuscular system and our attentive style develop along the same timeline.

Visual attention is a system that constantly undergoes change. As our demand increases, our visual attention starts to collapse. A good example of collapsed attention can be made by looking at tennis players. When they are in the backcourt, they see the net, the lines, the other player, and the ball approaching them. However, when they have to chase hard after a shot, they typically see only the ball. They are not aware of where the lines are, or the net, or the other player. Just as easily as they collapsed attention, they restore it back to full attention for their next shot. We are neurologically wired to perform in this exact way.

Visually incompetent children subjected to the complexity of visually demanding classrooms commonly collapse visual fields of awareness (similar to a tennis player). Habituation of compressed awareness fields results in excessive attention shifts from stimulus to stimulus, as observed in children with a diagnosis of attention deficits. The important question to be asked is: "What causes the differences in attention patterns?" Unfortunately, this question is not being asked.

Recent neurometabolic research shows that poor readers show more stimulation to Broca's area (auditory), while successful readers are more activated in visual areas during reading. Successful readers recognize words by their visual characteristics, whereas poor readers attempt to decode repetitively and convert words into auditory entities before recognition. This is a more complex and less efficient way to learn. A good way to think of this is that poor readers become both the storyteller and the listener.

We utilize two common types of attention. Transient attention is the ability to move our attention between two or more objects. This is a reflexive-based system. This system is a bottom-up system, starting at the level of the midbrain and cerebellum and ultimately reaching cortical areas of the brain.

Sustained attention is the other type of attention system. This is our ability to fixate on an object. This system is a slow, conscious system, starting at the level of the cortical areas of the brain and going down to the midbrain-cerebellar areas. On the basis of this observation, our magno system drives our attention more than our parvo system does. We also realize that we move attention first, then move our eyes.

For more information on this subject, visit the following Web sites:

http://www.optometrists.org

http://www.covd.org

http://www.visionandlearning.org

http://www.simplybrainy.com

http://www.pave-eye.com

http://www.oep.org

http://www.nora.cc

Charles Shidlofsky, OD, attended the University of Texas at Austin and the Southern College of Optometry, where he received the degrees of bachelor of science and doctor of optometry, respectively. He is a member of the College of Optometrists in Vision Development and the Neuro-Optometric Rehabilitation Association. Currently, he practices at the Neurodevelopmental Sensory Enhancement Center in Plano, Texas. Visit his Web site at www.dr-s.net or e-mail him at dr-s@dr-s.net.

Vision: A Piece of the Puzzle in Sensory Processing Disorders—Part 2

Charles Shidlofsky, OD

In the previous article in this series, we covered the anatomy and neurology of vision and visual attention. Like a good house, these are the foundation upon which we can build the visual sensory model. In this article, we will get more specific about the visual process in children with sensory issues and how we test and treat this special group of patients.

Vision Is a Bimodal Process

The visual system is composed of two processes: a central or focal process and a peripheral or ambient process. The focal system consists of fibers from both the magno and parvo cells and ultimately leads from the macula to the visual cortex. The ambient system takes fibers primarily from the peripheral retina and ends in the brain stem. The ambient vision process matches visual information with kinesthetic, proprioceptive, vestibular, and tactile information and sets up the foundation of higher sensory function.

Visual Symptoms of Sensory Processing and Autism Spectrum Disorders

Lack of eye contact, staring at spinning objects or light, fleeting peripheral glances, side viewing, and difficulty attending to visual tasks are some very common visual symptoms in children with sensory processing difficulties. Additionally, these children also seem to have:

- Tactile defensiveness, tending to become overstimulated by touch
- Visual defensiveness, tending to avoid contact with specific visual input and oftentimes having hypersensitive vision
- Difficulty "holding still" visually, tending to scan visual information constantly and repetitively to gain meaning from it

These children will often have substantial vestibular-based problems. Many common vision problems are associated with vestibular problems. Some of the common vision problems seen here are vertical eye imbalance, eye turn, convergence insufficiency, eye movement problems, restricted visual fusion abilities, and sluggish focusing ability.

The Role of the Neurodevelopmental Optometrist as Part of the "Sensory Team"

A neurodevelopmental optometrist (sometimes known as a developmental or behavioral optometrist) is trained to consider vision as a process that involves perception; integration of vision with the senses of touch, sound, and movement; and integration of all of these senses with motor control. This specialist cares for patients with visual disorders affecting human function and works in tandem with others from different disciplines, such as educational psychology, neuropsychology, occupational therapy, physical therapy, and speech-language pathology. Treatment includes the use of lenses, prisms, vision training, and any other means within their licensure. It is important to note that relatively few optometrists, and virtually no ophthalmologists, are trained in this area of specialization.

To look for visual sensory integration issues, neurodevelopmental optometrists test many areas of the sensory systems and assess the following abilities.

Eye movement ability includes two primary eye movement skills for vision. "Pursuits" is a smooth eye movement that allows us to track something, such as a ball or a teacher across a classroom. "Saccadics" is the ability to move our eye from object to object. We use this important skill for reading. Difficulties with eye movement ability include moving one's head excessively when reading, skipping lines when reading, omitting or transposing words when reading, requiring a finger or marker to hold our place while reading, experiencing confusion during the return sweep phase of reading, experiencing illusionary text movement, and difficulty with ball sports.

Eye teaming skills are also vitally important. This is the ability of the eyes to converge (move together) and diverge (move apart), as well as move together from side to side. Oftentimes when there is a problem in eye teaming, an eye may be noticed turning in or out (either all of the time or some of the time).

Accommodation or focusing is the ability to focus the eyes smoothly and accurately. This includes the ability to focus from near to far and from far to near. Visual attention is also sometimes considered a focusing skill.

Eye-hand coordination is the ability to move our hands in reaction to some visual stimulus.

Balanced integration of vision with other sensory systems is vital for us to be able to move effectively through our world. Problems in this area may include delayed development of gross motor skills; decreased coordination, balance, and ball-playing skills; confusion of right and left; letter reversal errors when writing or reading; inconsistent directional attack when reading; inconsistent dominant handedness; and difficulty in tasks that require crossing the midline.

Visual perception is our ability to interpret visual information. It includes such elements as visual motor integration, closure, visual spatial skills, and shape and form constancy.

Refractive status refers to whether one is nearsighted, farsighted, or astigmatic (or a combination of these).

Allergy states are commonly seen in children with attentional problems, necessitating nutritional evaluation. The optometrist considers whether the children need a dietary analysis to better control allergy states.

Other sensory systems integrate with and are crucial for vision. They, too, are assessed to provide a strong understanding of the auditory, vestibular, and tactile/kinesthetic systems. In our office, we utilize a group of tests called Sensory View to evaluate these sensory systems and how cognitive processing relates to the vision system. Specifically, we test the center of gravity and the sway needed to maintain that center of gravity, separation of head movements from eye movements, conscious and unconscious eye movements, memory skills, and auditory noise levels.

Treatment of Visual Sensory Integration Problems

There are many potential ways to treat those affected with vision-based sensory integration problems. Many doctors take different approaches on the basis of their experience and expertise. Treatment may involve using lenses, prisms, and/or vision therapy to enhance vision skills.

Typically, my preference is the use of a special type of prism lenses I call "Therapeutic Visual Sensory Integration Lenses." With its unique characteristics, this type of lens is the only one that can affect one's balance and response to the environment. Typically, if we look at the individual's center of gravity, we can shift it by utilizing lenses. Additionally, we can alter the person's environment in such a way that he becomes more spatially aware of his surroundings. This change has an effect of decollapsing visual attention, decreasing focusing strain, and allowing smoother and more accurate eye movements. From a functional perspective, in the case of reading, words seem to be larger and more spread out, focusing strain decreases, head movement lessens, and eye movements are smoother. What makes the effect special is how it affects the other sensory systems in calming down hyperreactive responses. Sometimes we also add in additional powers to relax focus or to correct an eyesight problem, such as nearsightedness, farsightedness, or astigmatism.

Once vision-processing skills have improved with lenses, the individual can often "reeducate" the visual system to a point of normalization. Sometimes the person needs help with the reeducation process. This is when we introduce vision therapy. Vision therapy is a systematic group of activities that are introduced to enhance specific vision skills or processing skills. This is like occupational therapy, just directed at the vision system.

Additionally, we look at the other sensory systems and make appropriate referrals to resolve other sensory processing problems. For example, if the person has an allergy state or nutritional problem, we might refer her to an allergist or nutritionist. If an auditory processing problem is perceived, we can refer the person to an audiologist for more extensive testing, and then perhaps to a speech pathologist for therapy. If the person has a vestibular problem, then we might refer her to an occupational therapist for sensory integration training.

Ultimately, our goals for treatment are to organize visual space and gain peripheral stability so that the patient can better attend to and appreciate central vision. At the same time, we hope to help the individual gain more efficient eye coordination and visual information processing.

Conclusion

Sensory processing disorders are multiple-system disorders that often mimic attentional issues. The diagnosis and treatment of visual sensory problems are ever evolving. New imaging techniques are making it possible to better understand the nature of how we take in information and learn. These same techniques are starting to be utilized to measure change in a system on the basis of a particular treatment. This so-called "evidence-based" medicine is evolving as an accepted way to look at data and measure change.

Hope is certain for children who have been having substantial classroom difficulties and were unable to be helped in the past because of misdiagnosed or undiagnosed visual processing problems. The most important fact is that vision is decidedly a piece of the sensory processing problem. I definitely advocate use of a multidisciplinary team—occupational therapists, speech pathologists, physical therapists, nutritionists, neurologists, physiatrists, and neurodevelopmental optometrists—to most effectively manage sensory processing disorders in children.

For more information on this subject, visit the following Web sites:

http://www.optometrists.org
http://www.covd.org
http://www.visionandlearning.org
http://www.simplybrainy.com
http://www.pave-eye.com
http://www.oep.org
http://www.nora.cc

Feel free to contact my office, as well, for more information at (972) 312–0177, or visit my Web site at *www.dr-s.net*.

Charles Shidlofsky, OD, attended the University of Texas at Austin and the Southern College of Optometry, where he received the degrees of bachelor of science and doctor of optometry, respectively. He is a member of the College of Optometrists in Vision Development and the Neuro-Optometric Rehabilitation Association. Dr Shidlofsky practices in Plano, Tex, and can be reached by e-mailing dr-s@dr-s.net.

Where Have All the Psychologists Gone? The Absence of Mental Health Professionals in Sensory Processing Disorders Treatment and Research

Jennifer J. Brout, EdM, PsyD

I am a psychologist and the mother of a child with a sensory processing disorder (SPD). As the nature of my daughter's sensory modulation problems unfolded, I realized that my overrespon-sivity to noise, light, and movement was not unique. I was unaware that my difficulties had a name. SPD has affected my emotional, academic, and motor functioning for as long as I can re-call. Thankfully, the understanding of sensory integration dysfunction has advanced since I was a child, so that my daughter has benefited from treatments that were not available to me. It is also encouraging that current research findings are extraordinarily compelling and promise to pave the way for further studies (see Miller and the SPD Scientific Workgroup on *SPDnetwork.org*) Ironically, although I am a psychologist, finding a mental health practitioner skilled in treating the emotional and behavioral consequences of SPD continues to be an arduous challenge for us, as it is for most families dealing with SPD.

Since A. Jean Ayres published her work on sensory integration in 1972 and 1979, mental health professionals have taken a back seat regarding most aspects of the disorder. Rather than initiate their own research, they have criticized the work of occupational therapists (OTs) and have taken a "wait and see" attitude regarding the nature of sensory processing problems. Notably, however, an exception has been the "zero to three" community, in which researchers and practitioners rec-ognize the role of sensory processing within both typical and atypical development.[1-2] Recently, the Interdisciplinary Council on Developmental and Learning Disorders reclassified Regulatory Disorders as Regulatory–Sensory Processing Disorders in its *Diagnostic Manual for Infancy and Early Childhood*. This change reflects a strong and growing body of research supporting SPD as distinct from other disorders in which sensory processing problems are symptoms, such as autism, Asperger syndrome, schizophrenia, and Fragile-X syndrome.[3]

School psychologists who often work with OTs are usually familiar with SPD. Yet, while they are aware of the negative effects of sensory processing problems on a child's socioe-motional and academic functioning, they do not seem to view themselves as potential con-tributors to the research. While it is encouraging that psychologists refer out to OTs, it is discouraging that they do not envision their role in the treatment and research of SPD. For example, psychologists could be pioneering research addressing the specific ways in which sensory processing problems affect children and families, which would inform the ways in which they would counsel families. Mental health researchers and clinicians could also be studying ways in which various psychological techniques might work in conjunction with OT to augment treatment and/or to help children successfully manage their sensory-based processing difficulties.

Frustrated Families

It is not surprising, then, that more often than not, parents who are seeking help find themselves increasingly disheartened as they progress through a bevy of mental health professionals. Some psychologists "believe in SPD," while others do not. Often, a psychologist is well intentioned but inadvertently makes things worse. For example, misdiagnosis is common, since psychologists lack easy access to information about SPD. Most psychologists do not read OT journals, and a "language barrier" must be crossed, as OT includes a great deal of terminology with which most mental health professionals are unfamiliar. Misdiagnosis is particularly menacing, as it can easily result in inappropriate psychological and pharmacological interventions.

We must not characterize SPD as a "psychological disorder," but as a nervous system disorder with psychological consequences (such as anxiety, depression, social withdrawal, aggression, and learning problems). However, the mental health field *does not have a collection of data on how sensory issues affect various kinds of children psychologically,* and therefore, we *do not have a model for individual psychotherapy or family counseling.* Consequently, parents, children, and psychologists alike become more and more frustrated as sticker charts, time-outs, and even supportive counseling fail. In general, the mental health field has overlooked sensory processing problems as causal or transactional in psychology and behavior.

Time-out for Time-outs!

In the 21st century, the integration of biology and behavior is omnipresent. With the widespread use of psychopharmacological medications and brain imaging techniques, evidence is stronger than ever for biologic etiologies and constitutional vulnerabilities in psychiatric and developmental disorders. Yet, the behaviorist theories of the 20th century still dominate much of psychological treatment. Although the mental health community largely accepts that temperament is constitutional and that the parent-child attachment is integral to basic survival and development, many psychologists still rely upon *techniques* that arose from the notion that we are born a "blank slate."

These behavior modification techniques are embedded in the theory that human behavior can be molded by reward contingencies or the removal of privileges. Through this behaviorist lens, the mind and the body become bifurcated, and despite a widespread belief to the contrary, psychologists still use techniques based upon this notion. This is particularly counterintuitive regarding SPD, for which evidence of a physiological etiology is strong. Sticker charts may work on children who *are able to self-regulate* but who need incentive to behave in a desired manner. One can modify a person's *behavior* with rewards, but one cannot train the nervous system through this one-dimensional form of therapy.

What Should Psychologists Be Doing Now?

Psychologists should NOT practice sensory integration treatment but should work collaboratively with OTs to support the child's and the family's mental health needs. Further, psychologists should acknowledge the inappropriate nature of most behavioral techniques in relation to the child with SPD. Mental health professionals need to research new treatment modalities for older children that are more in sync with the infant/child work that addresses sensory issues within the attachment relationship (taking emotion, physiology, and their interconnection into account). Psychologists could also begin to integrate other forms of psychologically based therapies with OT sensory integration treatment to further support regulatory capacities. For example, cognitive strategies (and the building of metacognitive skills) may be especially promising for a subset of children with SPD who have cognitive and/or verbal capabilities in average or above-average ranges.

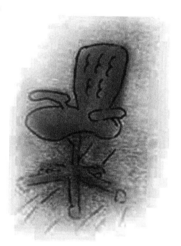

To develop effective treatment methods, mental health researchers and clinicians will need to pull from educational, counseling, cognitive, developmental, and clinical psychology. They will also need to gain a working knowledge of sensory processing and applicable neuroscientific functioning. This is a tall order, which will require assembling a new body of research and clinical experimental work. This will take time. Unfortunately, the urgency for mental health practitioners to become involved seems best understood by the large numbers of families who need psychological support, not by the practitioners or researchers themselves.

Yet, this is an extraordinary and exciting proposition for the mental health field that opens up entirely new avenues of research that may contribute to a much more comprehensive understanding of the developing child. When this happens, it is likely that a more integrated understanding of the child will emerge, which will inform both OT sensory integration treatment and psychological treatment of individuals and families affected by SPD.

References

1. DeGangi GA, DiPietro JA, Greenspan SI, Porges SW. Psychophysiological characteristics of the regulatory disordered infant. *Infant Behav Dev.* 1991;14:37–50.

2. Williamson GG, Anzalone ME. *Sensory Integration and Self-Regulation in Infants and Toddlers: Helping Very Young Children Interact with Their Environment.* Washington, DC: Zero to Three: National Center for Infants, Toddlers and Families; 2001.

3. Miller LJ. Empirical evidence related to therapies for sensory processing impairments. *NASP Communique.* 2003;31(5):34–37.

Mental health practitioner refers to psychologists, psychiatrists, social workers, and counselors.

For research supporting SPD as a physiologic disorder, please see the Scientific Workgroup studies at *www.SPDNetwork.org.*

I respectfully acknowledge Dr Lucy Miller and colleagues at the SPD Foundation for all they have done to advance the understanding of SPD and advocate for children with the disorder.

Jennifer J. Brout, EdM, PsyD, is a school/clinical psychologist in New York, who researches child and family therapy for children with SPD. She also volunteers for the SPD Foundation in a variety of professional capacities. She is a graduate of Columbia University and the Albert Einstein College of Medicine (Ferkauf School of Psychology).

Why Tommy Can't Comply: Overcoming the Obstacles of Medical and Environmental Considerations in Occupational Therapy

Rev. Kathleen R. Eickwort, PhD

I sat in the corner that afternoon and watched the occupational therapist work with my grandson. He was nearly 4 years old now and had started occupational therapy 2 years earlier. For some reason, he would not get on the platform swing or into the position she was asking him to. His sessions lately had deteriorated into a power struggle between therapist and child...and yet I knew this therapist to be a dedicated professional with an excellent reputation for sensory integration therapy.

Finally, she said to me, "I know he can do this, he's done it before." And to him, "Do you want to get on the swing or go to time-out?"

A pathetic little voice said, "Time-out."

While I watched her hold him, kneeling, in a basket restraint with his head down, my grandmotherly intuition said something was wrong. This child was not being defiant. Even if he had "done it before," I believed he could not tolerate that swing or comply with her requests at this moment. My suspicion, based on a personal and family history of food allergy, was that the underlying problem had something to do with the time of day and his school-controlled diet. A few weeks later, after consultation with Tommy's parents and Tommy himself, we discontinued occupational therapy, because it was not addressing the root problem.

My grandson Tommy had long-standing problems with vestibular dysfunction that may have started in the womb, where he could not move normally because of difficulties with his mother's placenta. He was born with congenital torticollis, with his head tipping to the right, and underwent physical therapy as an infant. At age 2, he was evaluated by a team of early-intervention specialists and found to have sensory integration dysfunction, receptive and expressive speech delay, and fine motor coordination problems. He has since been diagnosed with high-functioning autism. He had never been able to have a bowel movement, even once, sitting on a toilet or potty. He hated car rides in traffic, carousels, boats, and even the slowest amusement park ride. As a

2- to 3-year-old, he threw himself to the ground frequently, and, rather than walk, preferred to run to keep himself upright.

When he was enrolled in Head Start, his school would not allow any foods to be brought in from outside (because some children had peanut allergies), and so we could not provide a casein-free, gluten-free diet without a doctor's order. He did take digestive enzymes to alleviate any effects of food reactions, since they are very common in our family.

Some months after the incident in occupational therapy, I received a diagnosis of celiac disease. Before this, Tommy's pediatrician was not sympathetic to restricted diets. She said they were an "ugly way to live." But with this new information in the family history, she agreed that it would be good to find out if Tommy also had problems with gluten, because the digestive enzymes he was taking do not work alone for celiac disease. We opted to have EnteroLab do fecal serology (stool) tests, which are very sensitive and do not require a prescription or a blood draw. Tommy's antigliadin immunoglobulin A (IgA, an antigluten antibody) level was 24, with a "normal" range of 0-9. He also tested positive for anticasein IgA (antibodies against milk protein) and antitissue transglutaminase IgA (tTg). Anti-tTg is an autoantibody (an antibody against one's own tissues) produced specifically in individuals with celiac disease in reaction to the presence of gluten from wheat, barley, or rye (and sometimes oats). That autoantibody attacks not only the intestinal lining, but also the Purkinje cells in the cerebellum. Purkinje cells directly affect the vestibular functioning of the inner ear and are also involved in autism. And what had Thomas' school been giving him for his afternoon snack, right before his scheduled occupational therapy appointments? Cheese crackers! Almost certainly, he had been experiencing dizziness or nausea and was unable to communicate his discomfort to us.

Only in the past few years has gluten ataxia been researched and identified in the medical literature, mostly through the work of M. Hadjivassiliou, MD, and his colleagues in the United Kingdom. They found that in adults with "idiopathic sporadic ataxia" (translation: *idiopathic*—unknown cause; *sporadic*—coming and going; and *ataxia*—trouble with gait, balance, and vestibular function), 40% of them had serological antibodies typical of celiac disease, although in many cases, the adults did not have either the typical intestinal symptoms or the genetic human leukocyte antigen (HLA) type most common in classic celiac disease. (Patients with classic celiac disease with complete atrophy of the intestinal villi almost always have HLA-DQ2 or DQ8.) In fact, 22% of patients with gluten ataxia had HLA-DQ1, which both Tommy and I also have. All who maintained a gluten-free diet for a year recovered. Gluten can also cause problems with peripheral nerves, and so affect the tactile senses.

After his pediatrician read all these new medical journal articles, she called and told me that Tommy should not have even a single milligram of gluten. It was clearly a major cause of his vestibular difficulties.

Of course, for years, children on the autism spectrum have been restricted to gluten-free, casein-free (GFCF) diets because of the "opioid peptide" hypothesis—at least partially substantiated in many individuals—which states that wheat and milk proteins break down into peptides that connect with the brain's opiate receptors. Ingestion of gluten or casein puts the child into a kind of narcotic stupor. This of course could also lead to ataxia and vestibular problems, just as adults with ataxia are often mistakenly thought to be drunk, by the way they walk. Many children have done very well on GFCF diets, especially if started early in childhood. When the children stay on the diet, sensory and neurological functions improve; infractions have the opposite effect. Donna Williams, who was autistic as a child to the point where she did not speak understandably until the age of 9, says that for her, drinking milk was an LSD-type sensory experience, and high-salicylate foods caused a cocainelike drugging of her brain. She has IgA deficiency, as I do myself.

In Tommy's case, as soon as his pediatrician saw the test results, she assigned a diagnosis of celiac disease with neurological complications, and he went from taking digestive enzymes for gluten and casein (which had helped for a year) to being on an absolute, strict gluten-free diet. One immediate benefit made the inconvenience of the diet worthwhile: within 2 days, he was completely toilet trained, and he never had another soiling incident. His balance problems had been so severe that sitting on a toilet and relaxing was impossible. Another obviously vestibular turnaround was this: Before, he refused to go on a carousel or a boat ride, and he was often extremely uncomfortable in the car in traffic. Now, within a week after the gluten was removed from his diet, in a single day he went to a nearby theme park (where I had walked with him more than 20 times the previous year) and went on a boat ride, the merry-go-round, and the new Tower Ride with apparent enjoyment! He could walk without running, too. This weekend, after a year without gluten, he rode every ride at Lowry Park Zoo, and enjoyed riding a horse, as well. He now is also riding a bicycle without training wheels.

In any kind of therapy, especially with young children, distinguishing accurately between skill (ability) and compliance (performance) issues is crucial. In the case of speech therapy, hearing ability must be assessed before therapy is initiated, and this is policy for all early intervention. An attempt to force performance when a child is really unable to comply without extreme discomfort could lead to oppositional defiant disorder or to depression and a sense of failure. If a child cannot hear, his or her communication difficulties must be addressed in a different fashion from that used with hearing children. And although hearing may fluctuate, it probably does not do so as dramatically or rapidly as food reactions may cause balance problems.

I believe that children should be screened for gluten sensitivity, either by a careful trial of a GFCF diet or by serological tests, before they are expected to engage in occupational therapy for sensory vestibular dysfunction. Some occupational therapists already require that patients on the autism spectrum have GFCF diets, or they will not accept them. In any case, a noninvasive serological test that can be done on a stool specimen (in addition to a test of total IgA because the test will be inaccurate if the child is IgA deficient) should be required. Another alternative is a sensitive saliva test for gluten sensitivity. At the very least, therapists should be aware that a client's ability may vary and even show sudden dramatic deterioration depending upon diet. The frequent focus on vestibular functioning in sensory integration therapy makes gluten ataxia a particularly important clinical entity.

About 8% of autistic children in one study had IgA deficiency, which makes them more likely to have celiac disease and other food sensitivities, as well. The number of children who react to gluten with vestibular dysfunction, like gluten ataxic adults, is likely much higher among occupational therapy clients than the number of deaf prospective speech therapy clients, and much more likely to be undetected. Screening with sensitive tests for total serum IgA , anti-gliadin IgA and IgG, and tTg would help prevent situations where a child is unfairly blamed for something he cannot help. Even more important, screening may yield those individuals who can be helped by a gluten-free diet at an early age, before autoimmune or other gluten reactions may cause irreversible developmental problems due to loss of the Purkinje cells. It is a practice that would be valuable to adopt as a policy in occupational therapy practices, just as speech therapists require testing for adequate hearing. As a grandmother and an advocate for children, I would like to encourage the readers of *S.I. Focus* to seriously consider adopting this policy for their own children, and if they are occupational therapists or physicians, for the children in their practice.

Of course, gluten sensitivity is not the only food or chemical sensitivity problem that could affect brain functioning. Sensitivity to other foods is often reported in IgA-deficient individuals whose incomplete immune system makes sensitization—even multiple chemical sensitivities—likely. IgA is the immune system's primary defense in the mucosal membranes of the gut and respiratory system. For decades, allergists have recognized a symptom called "cerebral allergy" or "allergic tension-fatigue." People with another group of medical conditions may not tolerate ordinary amounts of sugars like lactose, fructose, or sucrose. Occupational therapists should be aware that their clients' skills and abilities or apparent compliance may vary from session to session for medical and environmental reasons. It might be helpful for therapists to give a checklist to parents to fill out regarding any change in diet, supplements, or the environment (is the interior of the house or the school being painted?) to assess the causes of any sudden regressions. The regressions may be a matter not of psychological or developmental changes, but of an environmental and medical neurobiological nature.

Let's not just blame the victim, who may be doing the best he can, even if it is not as well as he did last week!

References

1. Lieberman S, Segall L. *The Gluten Connection: How Gluten Sensitivity May Be Sabotaging Your Health—And What You Can Do to Take Control NOW.* New York, NY: Rodale Press; 2007.

2. Williams D. *Exposure Anxiety—The Invisible Cage: An Exploration of Self-Protective Responses in the Autism Spectrum and Beyond.* London, England: Jessica Kingsley Publishers; 2003.

3. Hadjivassilou M, Grunewald RA, Davies-Jones GAB. Gluten sensitivity as a neurological illness. *J Neurol Neurosurg Psychiatry.* 2002;72:560–563.

4. Hadjivassilou M, Grünewald RA, Chattopadhyay AK, et al. Clinical, radiological, neurophysiological, and neuropathological characteristics of gluten ataxia. *Lancet.* 1998; 352(9140):1582–1585.

5. Jennings JSR, Howdie PD. New developments in celiac disease. *Curr Opinion Gastroenterol.* 2003;19(2):118–129.

Useful Links

www.enterolab.com for gluten sensitivity stool and gene panel, which may be done with or without a doctor's prescription

www.immunoscienceslab.com for salivary gluten sensitivity testing with a prescription (see celiac disease antibody panel)

Since neurological manifestations of gluten sensitivity can be present without change in the small bowel villi, small-bowel endoscopy and biopsy results cannot rule out gluten ataxia. These tests are less specific for celiac disease but more sensitive for any gluten sensitivity.

The Rev. Kathleen Eickwort has a PhD in biology from Cornell University and worked for 6 years as a research associate in the Division of Nutritional Sciences there. She is a retired Episcopal priest and currently assists in the care and education of her grandson. She is currently working on another article on the role of vestibular stimulation (swinging, riding in a vehicle) in facilitating reading fluency in children with autistic spectrum disorder. If anyone has any anecdotal observations or knowledge of other research in this area, please contact her at Kathleen_E@usa.net.

Printing: The Foundation of Literacy

Cris Rowan, OTR

"Do we still need to teach our children to print?" As a pediatric occupational therapist, I'm frequently asked this question. The answer is unequivocally, "Yes!" Recent advances in technology have mistakenly led parents and teachers into thinking that computers will solve all children's problems, taking the place of printing, math, and even basic learning skills. On the contrary, recent studies show that technology is actually impeding children's ability to learn.

Technology has so invaded our culture that North American children now use TV, videogames, and computers 6.5 hours per day on average, resulting in physical and emotional development delays, attention difficulties, and poor school performance. Parents and teachers, as well as children, must come together and redefine basic learning objectives, so that all children can attain basic literacy in reading, printing, and math skills.

Many teachers and parents share the opinion that while reading is still an essential skill, printing is not. Many elementary-school teachers actually believe that the use of computers will replace learning to print. Subsequently, teachers do not emphasize or spend a lot of time teaching this essential skill. What these well-meaning teachers do not understand is that learning to print is a precursor for reading, spelling, and sentence formation. Therefore, if a child cannot print, that child is functionally illiterate.

Children have expressed tears, frustration, and embarrassment as they describe their diffi-culties in learning how to print. Marvin Simner, PhD, a professor with the University of Alberta, reports that printing has a "personal tone" for all children, and if a child's printing is low quality, it has a direct effect on that child's self-esteem. Dr Simner goes on to say in his book, *Promoting Skilled Handwriting,* that letter recognition, an important component in reading-skill acquisi-tion, develops primarily through a child's observations of his own attempts at letter formation, supported by repetitive practice and observation of the teacher or parent. Printing is therefore a *visual* and a *motor* task and requires practice of both components for skill achievement.

A good example would be a child who watches a soccer game on TV but is not able to go out and replicate the motor components necessary to have good soccer performance. This child needs to practice the motor components over and over again before a "motor plan" is formed. Once a child achieves a motor plan for a specific task, the task becomes subconscious, requiring very little cognitive attention for completion.

As printing is a motor task, the motor plan for each letter and number needs to be firmly estab-lished for that child then to be able to free up conscious thought for tasks such as reading, spelling, and sentence production. Children who are slow in establishing a motor plan for letter and number production or who have *inconsistent* motor plans—such as making their letters different ways—spend an inordinate amount of conscious mental energy in letter formation, leaving very little men-tal energy left for the creative thought required for reading, spelling, and sentence production.

When a child watches her hand and pencil make a letter or a number, this image is embedded in her visual memory, like a photograph taken with a camera. For proficiency in letter and num-ber production, many visual images of the correct motor plan need to be firmly embedded in the child's visual memory for reading, spelling, and sentence production to proceed smoothly. This process requires extensive time devoted by both parents and teachers in showing children a con-sistent method for letter and number production, with ample opportunity for practice. Failure to do so results in childhood illiteracy.

Often, teachers and parents mistakenly think that printing and reading skills can be achieved through printing workbooks, computer programs, or even TV programs, such as "Sesame Street" or "Baby Einstein."

Regarding workbooks: Although they do provide a visual image and opportunity for the child to practice letter and number production, workbooks do not "show" the child the proper place to start, which way to turn, and when to stop during letter formation. The "where and when" of printing letters is an integral piece in helping the child to form a subconscious motor plan and is the area of greatest skill deficit in children who have printing and reading difficulties. Just as children's physical development starts with their trunk and moves outward, stroke and shape production starts with big movements that use the whole body. Big movements teach directionality, laterality, and spatial skill components, which are necessary precursors to attempting letter and number production. Due to their sedentary lifestyles today, many children have not established the necessary trunk and shoul-der muscle control to be able to print. Only when a child's trunk is strong and his shoulder is mobile and stable can he position his wrist and hand to hold a pencil for printing.

Regarding educational or remedial-based computer and television programs: A two-dimensional screen image is considerably different from three-dimensional "real" life. Printing and reading are motor tasks, using the fine motor muscles of the eyes and hand, and should be taught as one would teach a sport. Optimal fine motor–skill development follows specific parameters, such as ensuring good trunk development prior to using the hand, accomplishing big movements before progressing to small movements, and ensuring adequate spatial concepts by starting with strokes and shapes before moving on to more complex letters and numbers. Meeting these essential printing and reading instructional parameters requires movement and motor skill practice. Relying on computer or television programs alone will not work.

Just as we have large muscles to control our trunk, arms, and legs, we also have small ocular muscles that control our eyes. To develop properly, the ocular muscles require stimulation to the brain's vestibular system. The vestibular system is the foundation for a child's ability to coordinate both sides of her body and eyes, to maintain erect posture, and to optimize arousal states necessary for learning. Because TV, videogames, and computers have small screens and are two-dimensional, children are not receiving adequate ocular muscle movement necessary for printing and reading. Developmental optometrists have reported a dramatic increase over the past 20 years in children with learning difficulties who have poor oculomotor coordination.

The point is: Use 'em or lose 'em! Children must develop and use their bodies and eyes the way nature intended, not with their bodies stuck on a chair and their eyes glued to a workbook or electronic screen. To reverse this ominous trend, parents and teachers need to reduce TV, videogame, and computer use and increase a child's activities that involve moving the body. Only then can printing and reading skills develop properly. Playing outside and viewing three-dimensional nature is very different from viewing a nature program on TV!

In my workshops, I ask parent and teacher participants to print their names quickly and then to print their names backward. Frustrated and anxious, the adults comment about not knowing where to start, which way to go, or when to stop. I ask that all adults who work with children who have difficulty printing and reading to please consider the amount of effort and mental energy required for these skills and to realize that when a child has difficulty, it's not only frustrating, but it can can be extremely exhausting. By the time children with printing and reading difficulties reach third or fourth grade, they have often given up trying, resulting in statements such as, "Printing is boring," and "Reading is stupid."

The foundation of literacy, printing is a necessity of ordinary life. To jot down a grocery list, to write a birthday card, to inscribe a book, and, usually, to take notes at seminars, we need to print. If we're doing it, we'd better be teaching it! Indeed, if we want our children to achieve literacy in reading, printing, and math and to optimize academic performance, we must help them learn basic skill sets and provide ample opportunity to practice these essential skills.

Reference

1. Simner ML. *Promoting Skilled Handwriting: The Kindergarten Path to Meaningful Written Communication.* Ottawa, Canada: Canadian Psychological Association; 2003.

Cris Rowan, OTR, BScOT, BScBi, SIPT, is an approved provider for ACTBC, the American Occupational Therapy Association, and the Canadian Association of Occupational Therapists. Cris has recently developed two new educational programs, Zone'in and Move'in, for use in schools and at home. Zone'in is derived from sensory integration theory and helps children get their energy "Zone'in to Learn." Move'in is based on fine motor development theory and is designed to help children print and read by taking them on a "printing adventure." For more information, please see www.zonein. ca and her Web site for Sunshine Coast Occupational Therapy at www.suncoastot.com.

Food Sensitivities and Their Relationship to Behavior and Learning: A Case Study

Jeanne Anduri, OTR

Temple Grandin, PhD, once said, "All behavior springs from a reason, and all behavior is communication." This statement has been a foundational concept in my approach with my clients.

Over my 28 years in practice as an occupational therapist, I have worked with families who are puzzled by erratic behaviors their child may demonstrate. Oftentimes, the families' similar anecdotes are linked to specific food sensitivities.

Much has been in the press recently about food *allergies*. There is less information, however, regarding food *sensitivities*, which appear to be more common, although often overlooked.

The word *allergy* is derived from two Greek words, meaning "altered reaction." A food allergy produces an immediate reaction, usually to the skin or to the respiratory or digestive system. Peanuts, shellfish, and strawberries are examples of the most commonly known food allergens.

A food sensitivity is a delayed reaction to a food. The reaction may occur in as little as 30 minutes or can be delayed up to a day or two after a person ingests the irritant—a delay that makes sensitivities difficult to pinpoint.

The response is often behavioral, as well as physical. Behavioral characteristics include temper tantrums and aggression, hyperactivity, mood swings, food cravings, fatigue, depression, inflexibility, poor concentration, and whining. Some physical characteristics include red earlobes and cheeks in toddlers; dark circles under the eyes or puffy eyes; excessive nighttime perspiration; recurrent ear, sinus, and respiratory infections; and intestinal complaints, to name just a few.

Many symptoms of frequently diagnosed childhood issues (attention-deficit disorder, attention-deficit/hyperactivity disorder, autism, and sensory processing disorder) may be diminished by addressing potential food sensitivities. Dairy, wheat, nuts, corn, soy, yeast, food coloring, and preservatives are some of the most common triggers for children. My experience suggests that dairy, wheat, and food coloring are the first triggers to address. Food coloring can be particularly irritating to children who have tendencies toward hyperactivity. Something as simple as children's toothpaste that has food coloring can precipitate hyperactivity and make settling down for bedtime a challenge. However, given all the products that include food coloring, children may be ingesting the irritant throughout the day. Careful reading of all labels and eliminating products with added coloring can help to reduce hyperactivity.

Eliminating a specific food group for 5 days and then reintroducing it and observing the child's behavior can yield information helpful in determining if a food is an irritant and if the child is sensitive to it. If diet is not addressed as a potential contributing factor, incomplete diagnoses may be achieved on the basis of behavior alone. Often, medications are prescribed, and children are placed on Individual Education Plans (IEPs) at school. The problem behaviors may not be alleviated, and the medication may have additional deleterious effects on the child's behavior and ability to function.

The following case study illustrates how a food sensitivity is as critical to determine and prevent as a food allergy.

Four-month-old Deby seemed to be developing typically until her mother, Monica, introduced cereal. Monica became concerned when Deby's ear infections began. By 9 months, she was being given adult doses of antibiotics. She began to develop phobias shortly thereafter, beginning with hats. Next, the moon became frightening; the family couldn't go out at night and had to get rid of all books with hats and moons. The toilet was the next object of fear.

By the age of 4, Deby could identify the spectrum of colors, although she could not count and had no interest in singing the alphabet. By 5 years, she had imaginary friends that were scary people. She was held back from starting kindergarten until she was 6, at which time she was administered Ritalin for attention-deficit disorder. Monica did not believe this was an accurate diagnosis, and she felt the Ritalin created a flat affect in Deby's demeanor. Deby played alone, was lethargic, and didn't like to be held. Soon, cartoons became too scary to watch.

Her fears were compounding. She was afraid of thin, "bony" people, as well as clouds. By second grade, she would ask, "Mommy, do you think you might die today?"

Movement, however, did not frighten her. When the family went to Disney World when she was 6, Deby showed no expression of joy, except that she was happy when on a ride. When the ride ended, she was immediately flat again. Deby's sensory processing deficits and need for movement and other appropriate sensory input were evident but were overshadowed by the severity of her psychological condition.

Deby started experiencing visual and auditory hallucinations, which were increasingly violent. School was a terrifying experience on a daily basis.

Although she taught herself to play the flute, she could not read by fourth grade. Monica was told at this time that her daughter needed to be in a special behavior and discipline program. Her IEP indicated that she had a significant identifiable emotional disability.

Deby was out of touch with reality. She had excessive fears and anxiety. She demonstrated markedly limited self-control with impaired attention. She exhibited persistent physical complaints not caused by a medical condition. Deby went to the school nurse's office every day shortly after lunch, complaining of stomachaches and fever.

In September of 2004, at 8 years old, Deby was hospitalized for suicidal ideations, homicidal statements, visual and auditory hallucinations, and voices telling her to kill herself. Her physicians stated, "It appears she is chemically and psychologically unstable. She is anxious and demonstrates constant rocking, self-soothing behaviors."

Her medications thus far included Ritalin at age 6, which was discontinued because of increasing nightmares and anxiety. By the age of 8, she was diagnosed with obsessive-compulsive disorder; administered Paxil, which increased the frequency of psychotic episodes; hospitalized, and given Depakote and then Risperdal; and diagnosed with bipolar disorder, and given Xanax and then Tegretol.

Interestingly, Monica and two of her other children were gluten- and dairy-intolerant. They had all the typical symptoms of digestive distress, gas, bloating, and pain. All food served at home adhered to gluten- and dairy-free guidelines. Deby's symptoms were so unusual and her diet at home was so regulated, however, that Monica never suspected a food connection.

Deby was transferred to a private school for fifth grade. Monica was sending lunches from home, as there was no lunch program offered at the new school, and her teacher started noticing changes in Deby's behavior. On Fridays, however, school personnel took the kids to a restaurant for lunch, and every Friday, the symptoms would return. Initially, Monica thought going to the restaurant was overstimulating Deby. The hallucinations started to return. Deby would see people looking at her with red eyes, their hair on fire, and blood on their faces.

It was after a few of these recurrent Friday episodes that Monica made the food connection. She completely eliminated gluten and dairy from Deby's diet.

Within days, Monica noticed substantial improvement in Deby's behavior. The hallucinations, anxieties, and self-soothing behaviors ended.

Deby was able to return to a regular classroom, and by the next IEP meeting, she was no longer designated as having a significant identifiable emotional disability. Most notably, Deby has not been on any medication now for more than 2½ years.

Her social worker describes her process as incredible. Deby has blossomed. She is confident, learning well, and socially age appropriate and successful in school. She is now in seventh grade, a happy and healthy social being—and a parent's dream.

As a typical preteen, however, she is exposed to dairy and wheat when she goes out to eat occasionally with friends. Her symptoms are not as severe when she does eat the offending foods, since she remains gluten- and dairy-free on a daily basis. Now, her mother describes symptoms that exhibit within 8 hours after exposure as predictably manic. Deby either becomes depressed or giggles constantly, but the symptoms clear within the day.

Unfortunately, Deby's situation is not an isolated case. Since presenting her case at a conference, I have met others who have experienced severe psychological reactions and have completely cleared their symptoms on a gluten- and dairy-free diet, as well. The range of symptoms caused by food sensitivities is far-reaching. Symptoms may not always be as severe as Deby's, although they clearly have a substantial effect on the lives of those involved. Schoolwork, family life, and social connections are all affected when a child or adult has an unknown food sensitivity.

In my practice, Dr Temple Grandin's statement has been prominent. "All behavior springs from a reason, and all behavior is communication." Our task is to help decipher the reason behind the behavior, not simply to apply a label. Children communicate through their aggressive behavior, through stubborn behavior, through fearful behavior, and the list goes on and on.

If a child is diagnosed with a food allergy that has the potential to create a life-threatening consequence, a huge effort is put in place to prevent the exposure. We need to look at food sensitivities the same way.

My experience with families over the years has demonstrated that what we eat and put on our skin does have a very definite effect on our bodies and brains. Unfortunately, traditional physicians and allergists do not universally embrace the effect of food sensitivities. Several of Deby's physicians do not acknowledge the connection, even after 2½ years of her being symptom-free. Consider the possibilities of raising public awareness about the effect of food sensitivities! Children and adults could be like Deby, living full, productive, social lives.

For more information on food sensitivities and the effects on learning and behavior, check out the Center for Science in the Public Interest at *www.cspinet.org*, which has well-researched information, free of special interest–funded studies.

References

1. Grandin T. *Thinking in Pictures*. New York, NY: Doubleday; 1995.

2. Rapp D. *Is This Your Child? Discovering and Treating Unrecognized Allergies in Children and Adults*. New York, NY: William Morrow; 1991.

    More references are available upon request.

Jeanne Anduri, OTR, has been a practicing occupational therapist since 1979. She has consulted with families and seen remarkable personality and behavioral changes in children and adults for the past 17 years. She has most recently worked in the school system and is now employed in a sensory integration clinic in Denver. She can be reached at jeanneanduri@yahoo.com.

The Meaning of the Ayres Sensory Integration Trademark

Zoe Mailloux, MA, OTR/L, FAOTA;
Susanne Smith Roley, MS, OTR/L, FAOTA;
Brian W. Erwin

For some parents, a gut-wrenching moment comes when they realize that the unhappy or out-of-control behavior exhibited by their child could indicate a deeper problem. If they are lucky, someone in their community—a family member, teacher, friend, or healthcare professional—knows enough to recommend that their child be tested for sensory integration dysfunction. Otherwise, perhaps through their own research in books or on the Internet they can grasp an idea of their child's underlying difficulties.

In an ideal world, what happens next would not be confusing. Parents would be able to locate a therapist trained to test and provide therapy for this dysfunction, as defined by the researcher who created the assessment and intervention for these hidden disorders over 40 years ago, Dr A. Jean Ayres. Beginning in the 1960s, Dr Ayres systematically investigated the nature of the way the brain processes sensory information so that it can be used for learning, emotions, and behavior, and she created sensory integration theory as it is currently used in occupational therapy practice and applied in pediatrics and childhood education.

Unfortunately, due to U.S. copyright law, the term *sensory integration* is considered to be in the public domain. This means that almost anyone can offer almost any form of therapy and call it "sensory integration." While some of these forms of sensory integration therapy may be valid, some are not, or they lack the rigorous research necessary to back their claims.

For this reason, the trust created by Dr Ayres and her husband applied for and received a registered trademark—Ayres Sensory Integration—to protect the integrity of this specific definition and practice of sensory integration. To aid parents in locating therapists trained to test and provide therapy based upon Dr Ayres' theory, it is helpful to understand how it is defined. Then, parents will know what questions to ask prospective therapists.

The Ayres Sensory Integration Registered Trademark

The Ayres Sensory Integration trademark encapsulates:

- Dr Ayres' theory
- The assessment of sensory integration dysfunction and patterns of sensory integration and praxis (the process of getting the idea, initiating, and completing new motor tasks) dysfunction
- Intervention concepts, principles, and techniques, as applied by therapists trained in this approach worldwide

Sensory Integration Theory

Sensory integration theory, based upon Ayres' work, proposes that sensory integration is a process of the brain that organizes sensation from one's own body and from the environment and makes it possible to use the body effectively within the environment. The brain interprets, associates, and unifies all of these sensations, knowing what to do with it (eg, "step down from the curb"), as well as how to do it (eg, "move one leg forward first to step down"). It also includes knowing how to organize this information for what Ayres called "purposeful activity" (eg, "to cross the street, one must first step down from the curb").

A deficiency in the individual's ability to engage effectively in this transaction at critical periods interferes with optimal brain development and consequent overall ability. Identifying the deficient areas in a young person and addressing them therapeutically can enhance the individual's opportunity for normal development.

Evaluating Sensory Integration Dysfunction

Ayres developed 17 standardized tests and many nonstandardized observations that contributed to the identification and understanding of the multiple patterns of sensory integration dysfunction. Today, they are called the Sensory Integration and Praxis Tests (SIPTs).

Patterns of sensory integration dysfunction include sensory contributions to motor incoordination, fine and gross motor delays, deficits in balance, poor praxis, as well as unusual oversensitivity, undersensitivity, or fluctuating responses to sensation.

In practice, the SIPT is considered the standard of reference for assessing sensory integration dysfunction. It is intended for school-age children without severe motor or mental disorders. It may be used on older individuals. It is commonly used with children with a diagnosis of high-functioning autism or Asperger syndrome. For those individuals for whom the SIPT is not appropriate, other methods and assessments must be used to glean the information. Only professionals certified in SIPT are able to administer the test and evaluate the results.

Intervention Principles Based on Sensory Integration Theory

In 2002, occupational therapy experts from various sites across the United States together identified and defined the core principles of sensory integration intervention as used in professional practice, such as occupational therapy. The following 12 ingredients are deemed essential to the delivery of intervention with a sensory integration approach:

1. A qualified professional—be it an occupational therapist, physical therapist, or speech-language pathologist

2. A family-centered intervention plan, based on a complete assessment and interpretation of the patterns of sensory integrative dysfunction; collaboration with significant people in the individual's life; adherence to ethical and professional standards of practice

3. A safe environment, which includes equipment that will provide vestibular (a system in the body that is responsible for maintaining balance, posture, and the body's orientation in space), proprioceptive (for sensing the motion and position of the body), and tactile sensations, and opportunities for praxis

4. Activities rich in sensation, especially those that provide vestibular, tactile, and proprioceptive sensations and opportunities for integrating that information with other sensations, such as visual and auditory

5. Activities that promote regulation of affect and alertness and provide the basis for attending to salient learning opportunities

6. Activities that promote optimal postural, oral motor, and oculomotor control, including holding against gravity and maintaining control while moving through space

7. Activities that promote praxis, including organization of activities and self in time and space

8. Intervention strategies that provide the "just-right challenge"

9. Opportunities for the client to make adaptive responses to changing and increasingly complex environmental demands; highlighted in Ayres Sensory Integration intervention principles is the "somatomotor adaptive response," which means that the individual is adaptive with the whole body, moving and interacting with people and things in three-dimensional space

10. Intrinsic motivation and drive to interact through pleasurable activities—in other words, play

11. An atmosphere of trust and respect, engendered by the therapist through contingent interactions with the client (ie, activities are negotiated, not preplanned, and the therapist is responsive to altering the task, interaction, and environment on the basis of the client's responses)

12. An intrinsic reward in the activities and in the therapist's ensuring the child's success in whatever activities are attempted by altering them to meet the child's abilities

The current application of Ayres Sensory Integration is based on evidence from carefully designed studies that adhere to the intended principles, as well as extensive related neurobiological, psychological, and therapeutic research.

What a Parent Can Do

Ayres-based sensory integration theory, evaluation, and intervention is not ambiguous! It is a deeply researched form of evaluation and therapy in which professionals either are or are not trained. Your task as a parent seeking the right therapist for your child can be made easier by doing the following:

Read Dr Ayres's book, *Sensory Integration and the Child* (Western Psychological Services, 2006). Her explanation of her theory mirrors the same language she used when conferring with parents of the children for whom she was providing therapy. It is written in her careful and caring voice.

Visit the Sensory Integration Global Network Web site at *www.siglobalnetwork.org*. The content on this site was written and compiled by many of the finest researchers and clinicians of Ayres Sensory Integration.

Take a copy of this article with you when you interview therapists. Have them explain how their practice complies with the 12 "Intervention Principles Based on Sensory Integration Theory."

By selecting your therapist carefully, you can hasten the powerful process of completing the integration of your child's brain. As therapists and as parents who have experienced this, we can assure you that better days lie ahead.

Zoe Mailloux, MA, OTR/L, FAOTA, is the director of administration at the Pediatric Therapy Network. Susanne Smith Roley, MS, OTR/L, FAOTA, is project director for the University of Southern California/Western Psychological Services (USC/WPS) Comprehensive Program in Sensory Integration, USC Division of Occupational Science and Occupational Therapy. Brian W. Erwin is a successor trustee of the Franklin B. Baker/A. Jean Ayres Baker Trust and a parent.

From Arousal to Action: The Neurobiology of Challenging Behavior

Kimberly Barthel, BMR, OTR

Is challenging behavior a sensory processing problem, or is it just "bad behavior"? This question was recently asked in the New York Times and will continue to be posed repeatedly to therapists and researchers alike. The answer to why people behave the way they do demands a wider frame of awareness than the question of, "Is it simply one thing or another?" Many overlapping, integrating, and continuum-related factors contribute to the complex reasons why challenging behaviors arise. Collectively, various influencing factors gather inside the nervous system as neurochemistry and are translated into a state of "arousal" or internal energy that underpins the drive to act or react. It is this arousal state that we must learn to observe, identify, and evaluate as a backdrop behind the scenes of behavioral interaction.

With the help of rapidly expanding neuroimaging technology, cellular neurobiology, and pharmacology, windows of knowledge are opening that provide expansive insights into the relationship between the brain and human behavior. This appreciation of the workings of the human brain supports the realization that all behavior is purposeful and functional in nature. This view shifts professionals and parents away from the idea that challenging behavior is "manipulative" or "intentional" to a different perception—one that elicits compassion and a desire to understand what a behavior means.

How Is Arousal Related to Action?

When we talk about "arousal" in neurophysiology, we are describing the state of the brain's neurological activity—the level of excitability within the nervous system.

This level of background activity within the nervous system is adaptable and flexible. This flexibility allows for modifiable adjustments of both internal activity within the body and behaviors necessary to engage with the varying demands of the environment. Arousal gets us ready for action!

Typical nervous systems are flexible enough to allow for participation in a broad spectrum of tasks, from sitting and watching television to sky-diving and mountain-biking. Each person has his own "comfort zone," or an optimal range where his best performance occurs. It is also a range to which the nervous system tries to return when an environmental event (stressor) has sent arousal beyond the comfort zone. Some of us function best at the lower end of the range, while others may need to be in a higher range to function comfortably.[1]

Arousal is viewed as a continuum, ranging from sleep through alert wakefulness to states of emotional tension. Increases in arousal make behavior more stereotypical (predictable and the same), and decreases in arousal make behavior more variable and flexible.[2]

How Is Arousal Created in the Brain?

How, then, does the brain regulate itself? The maintenance of attention and appropriate arousal is no small accomplishment, requiring integration of many different structures of the nervous system. Excitatory (stimulating) and inhibitory (quieting) mechanisms in the brain work together to tease out what is important enough for the individual's attention.

The communication system of the brain relies upon chemical messengers to deliver the information. Five distinct neurochemical systems work together in the brain to increase arousal. These systems use the neurotransmitters norepinephrine, dopamine, serotonin, acetylcholine, and histamine as messengers. As these chemicals work together, a symphony of activity is orchestrated inside the brain, creating meaning out of the thoughts, feelings, and sensory stimuli we perceive from the world around us.

Sensation Affects Arousal

We all know that the brain takes in sensory stimulation through the sensory receptors (eyes, ears, nose, skin, etc) and that these data feed the brain with information that stimulates wide-reaching components of the brain's networks. The appropriate registration, filtration, orientation, interpretation, and integration of these data are necessary for appropriate function and action! When sensory processing does not work well, dramatic behavioral responses are often observed, suggesting a mismatch between sensory perception and the environmental demands.

At the most basic level of brain processing, information from the senses makes a stopover in a structure called the *reticular formation*. The weblike cluster of neurons sends signals to far-reaching parts of the brain, influencing the general sense of alertness. Through the reticular formation, sensation has a profound effect upon the arousal system of the brain. The primary purpose of this stopover in the reticular formation is for *survival* purposes. Pain, light touch, head movement, smell, sound, and light signal survival messages that demand greater attention than other stimuli. It is the reticular formation that first hears the alarm clock blast in the morning, creating a cascade of adrenaline that results in a startle reaction and a potential hop out of bed. It's also the structure that magnifies the sound of footsteps as you walk through a dark alley, alerting you to the possibility of a "saber-toothed tiger" or a stalker behind you.

The intensity, duration, and frequency of a sensory stimulus can also affect the reticular formation. Stronger or more intense stimuli generally have an alerting effect on the reticular formation, whereas gentler stimuli can be soothing and calming, reducing the overall level of arousal. Increased frequency and duration of stimulation can result in the nervous system's *habituation* to data, resulting in a diminished alerting response to the information presented. Those of us who are addicted to coffee know what this habituation response is like. That one cup of java no longer has the punch it once had; we need more and more to experience the same effect. Manipulating sensory variables can be an effective strategy in preparing the client to learn a new skill by influencing the background state of arousal—waking up the brain.

The reticular formation is a front-line defense, acting like a filter on your air conditioner. This structure prevents irrelevant stimuli from passing on to higher structures of consciousness, so that only the most important sensory cues are interpreted. Two-way telephone conversations between the reticular formation and higher-order structures of the brain modulate the data coming from the brain stem. Through this communication, attention is sharpened or dampened. Many clients with neurological impairment experience challenges in their ability to filter out the irrelevant information bouncing around inside the nervous system. This sensory information, entering the brain from the "bottom" and traveling upward toward the cortex for interpretation, is known as "bottom-up" processing of arousal energy.

Cognition Affects Arousal

Have you ever awakened suddenly at 3 o'clock in the morning, worrying about something? In the absence of any sensory stimulation, you can *think* your way into a state of chaos. This is an example of cognition influencing your state of arousal. Another example is when you have a paper due tomorrow at school and, even though you are tired, you are *motivated* to get it done. The adrenaline from the time pressure may give you the state of arousal necessary to complete your task.

Cognition helps decide, sharpen, and accentuate arousal through top-down brain networks. For example, when you read a chapter in a book and it is very exciting, the top of your brain (cortex) sends a message down to the bottom of your brain (reticular formation) to dampen other stimuli, ensuring you will stay focused on the interesting story. Together, bottom-up and top-down influences merge for the creation of a "just-right" state of arousal in relationship to task. Action is controlled by both motivation and cognition.

Reward pathways in the brain are also critical for survival and action, resulting in a repetition of a previously experienced stimulus. "Natural rewards" release dopamine (a neurochemical) in the brain, resulting in feelings of pleasure and comfort. The same cells in the brain that signal reward under natural conditions can also release dopamine and feelings of pleasure with "unnatural rewards," such as alcohol, cocaine, and nicotine, and by compulsive activities, such as gambling, binging, risk-taking behaviors, and other addictions. These reward cells arouse the brain, telling the person that something exciting is going on. It is brutally clear that in a monotonous environment, lacking change, a human will lose arousal and will become less alert. When clients are bored or mismatched in arousal state to environmental demands, conditions arise where challenging behavior is likely to occur.

The brain has a structure designed specifically for noticing something new! This "novelty detection" center is known as the *locus coerulus* and receives an abundance of sensory data from the reticular formation. The novelty center shouts loudly to the rest of the brain when a new stimulus is presented in the environment. Uniquely, this structure is the only source of noradrenaline (up-regulation) in the neocortex of the brain, heightening arousal, creating vigilance, and modulating the body's stress response. Unpredictable, changing, and new stimulation keeps the brain aroused and interested. Many clients need this level of novelty to generate a "just-right state" of arousal. Video games, fast-moving activities, and risk-taking actions may, in fact, be used to alter the dial on a low level of arousal, as they attempt to adjust their chemistry to an optimum state. Additional ways to up-regulate arousal must be explored to help an individual expand his range of activities beyond the computer and danger-seeking behaviors.

Arousal levels are highly influenced by cognitive task complexity. Optimal performance typically occurs at medium levels of arousal, allowing concentration without stress. When a task becomes too hard, arousal levels elevate stress outside of the zone of optimum learning comfort, diminishing performance. Alternately, simple, mundane tasks need higher levels of arousal within the brain to sustain interest; for example, increasing the speed or adding a reward for the performance of a repetitive task will elicit higher levels of arousal within the nervous system. Challenging behaviors are often observed when the cognitive demands of a task exceed an individual's cognitive capacity. Evaluating an individual's cognitive skills in relation to a task is a critical aspect of the overall assessment of the challenging behavior. If a task is too difficult for a client to comprehend, negative behavioral outcomes may be observed as an attempt to avoid the task presented. Cognitive mismatch between intellectual capacity and task can markedly alter overall arousal, driving behavior into a negative space and communicating discomfort.

The frontal cortex (thinking brain) makes decisions, moderates emotions, compares information in memory, links concepts, and makes judgments about how to act in relationship to the environment. Specifically, the right orbital frontal cortex (OFC) is directly involved in the neurological processes of arousal and attention. The job of the OFC is to decide which aspect of a stimulus is appropriate for focused attention. The right OFC is designated to interpret the emotional content of the communications—the other person's body language, eye movements, and tone of voice. It gathers data about the emotional context of a situation. The OFC also monitors impulse control, helping to inhibit the lower centers in the brain where urgent emotional drives originate. This part of the brain is an example of top-down influences on the arousal system of the brain.

When it is working smoothly, the OFC can delay emotional reactions long enough to allow mature, more sophisticated behavioral responses to arise. When its connections are disrupted, it lacks this capacity. Individuals who have experienced neurological damage to the right OFC demonstrate behaviors classic to attention-deficit disorder, autistic spectrum disorder, Asperger syndrome, and other neurological disorders. Without this monitoring effect of the OFC, impulses and dampening of arousal responses become less available. The right OFC grows rapidly and substantially at the onset of puberty, continuing on well into a person's 20s and perhaps even their 30s. As cognition matures and develops, self-reflection, self-awareness, and behavioral monitoring expand in their top-down inhibition of the potentially arousing effects of emotional and sensory influences. Cognition can be engaged to soothe or enhance the brain's arousal activity.

Emotion Affects Arousal

Sensation and cognition are not the only variables that contribute to our levels of arousal in the nervous system. Emotional reactions also juice up and regulate this state of being. The nervous system, which is something akin to a bucket of chemicals, does not clearly differentiate whether the neurochemical experience is caused by a sensory stimulus or an emotional reaction to a situation. Because our brain is wired for survival, intense emotional experiences become rapidly hardwired in our neural nets to remind us to seek or avoid that experience again.

Different emotions are produced by different parts of the brain. Varying amounts of arousal energy are available to the mind and body and are dependent upon the emotion elicited by a stimulus. Sensory stimuli or experiences that elicit fear will provide greater amounts of arousing information to the brain, increasing the opportunity for that information to become hard-wired in memory faster and more prominently. If the tags in my shirt are an identifiable sensory stimulus paired with a fear emotion, all I will have to do is "think" about the tags in my shirt, and a flood of arousal chemistry will fill my brain as if the experience were happening in the now.

The right OFC, or the top-down controller of emotions, has also been clearly identified as the brain structure of attachment and relationship. Neuroimaging performed in parents and babies has demonstrated a brain-wave attunement that occurs during this feeling of connection and has been identified as *attachment*. This brain-wave synchrony between parents and their babies in the right OFC sets the stage for stable regulation of this arousal and attentional center of the brain. Relationships help regulate and organize the brain for learning, helping the person regulate and modulate her behavior. Through practice and repeated connection, babies learn to regulate their own brains and carry this pattern into their future relationships. Individuals with challenging behaviors need healthy relationships to assist them in accessing this critical part of their brain.

The up-regulation and down-regulation of emotionally driven behavior depends upon patterns of autonomic and hormonal adaptations. Autonomic arousal plays an important part in the story of behavior. The autonomic nervous system is divided into two parts: *sympathetic* and *parasympathetic* systems. Sympathetic autonomic neurons use norepinephrine as their messenger, using metabolic energy to prepare the body for action. In contrast, the parasympathetic autonomic responses work primarily through the vagus nerve, using acetylcholine as their messenger, with the goal of preserving metabolic energy for when it is needed.

Every experience in life has an emotional overlay associated with that experience. It takes only one trial to learn that being bit by a dog is scary and dangerous—survival depends upon it. Trauma, sensation, and physiology become coded as one inside the mind and body. Remembering a previous experience will instantaneously conjure image, thought, and emotion holistically as a unified encounter that is coded as neurochemical networks in the brain.

Many of our clients do not have harmonious interactions between the tops and the bottoms of their brains! Some are hyperreactive and sensitive in their state of arousal. They may be stuck in constant "survival" mode, alerted to the feeling of the lint in their socks, the sounds of fluorescent lights, and many other sensations that are typically in the background of our consciousness. When the brain's attention is directed towards these innocuous data, focus is taken away from other data. Other clients may be hyporeactive, not attending to the environment at all or altering their behavioral reactions to the world around them, even when faced with danger.

Hence, we discover that complex, challenging behavior arises from mixed influences of our thoughts, feelings, and sensations that merge inside us, producing actions that are based upon these states. Evaluating complex behaviors demands that therapists consider sensory processing, cognitive capacity, and emotional regulation when developing optimum interventions and supports for challenging behavior.

How Do We Decide What Is Going On?

Therapists need to focus on the process of understanding challenging behaviors by examining the factors that set the stage for these actions and the functions that they serve. *What the behavior looks like* is less important than *what function the behavior serves.* Through the detective process, the therapist identifies the variables that motivate and maintain challenging behaviors. Some of the functions that challenging behavior serves are *(a)* obtaining connection and affiliation, *(b)* obtaining objects or skills, *(c)* avoiding and/or escaping pressure, demand, or limitations, and *(d)* gaining sensory input.

Therapists need to consider *setting events* that have occurred in the past. Setting events set the stage for a challenging behavior but do not directly trigger them; these events do not occur directly before the behavior. For example, inadequate sleep, side effects of medications, previous negative interactions with service providers, or gastrointestinal problems are all examples of "stage setters" that load the arousal system with influencing neurochemistry. *Antecedent stimuli* that occur just before a behavior directly trigger a challenging behavior and also need to be evaluated. Examples of antecedent stimuli are a service provider's demands, a loud noise in the hallway, someone touching you unexpectedly, or an interruption in an expected routine.

Consequent stimuli occur immediately after a behavior has occurred. Examples of consequent stimuli include gaining connection or attention from a person, escaping from an uncomfortable situation, or meeting a sensory need. Through interview, direct observation, and experimental manipulation of antecedents and consequences, the "meaning" behind the scenes is revealed.[3]

The detective process unveils the variables guiding the creation of holistic and meaningful intervention strategies, which include sensory, cognitive, and emotional components. In the quest to understand why humans act the way they do, neurobiology provides a reinforcing link, emphasizing the blend of forces that creates the complexity of human action. It is no longer a simple question of, "Is the behavior sensory or just bad behavior?"

References

1. Oetter P, Richter E, Frick S. *M.O.R.E.: Integrating the Mouth with Sensory and Postural Functions.* Stillwater, MN: PDP Press; 1995:29–30.

2. Sternberg R. *Handbook of Creativity.* New York, NY: Cambridge University Press; 1998: 137–145.

3. Mu K, Gabriel L. Comprehensive behavior support: strategies to cope with severe challenging behavior. *OT Pract.* 2001;January 22:12–17.

4. Frick S, Hacker C. *Listening with the Whole Body.* Madison, WI: Vital Links; 2001.

5. Williamson GG, Anzalone ME. *Sensory Integration and Self-Regulation in Infants and Toddlers: Helping Very Young Children Interact with Their Environment.* Washington, DC: Zero to Three; 2001.

Kim Barthel, BMR, OTR, is an author, consultant, occupational therapist, and owner of Labyrinth Journeys, a company dedicated to providing professional and personal growth workshops. Kim is a neurodevelopmental treatment OT instructor and a teacher of sensory integration therapy.

Focus on Research: Advocating for Recognition of DSI Progress in DSI Research

Lucy Jane Miller, PhD, OTR; Barbara Brett-Green, PhD

2010 UPDATED INTRODUCTION

Lucy Jane Miller, PhD, OTR; Sarah A. Schoen, PhD, OTR; Darci M. Nielsen, PhD

Five years ago, in 2004, *S.I. Focus* published an article summarizing our research in sensory integration that was growing by leaps and bounds. Now, 5 years later, progress has far exceeded our expectations. This short introduction serves as an update on important research developments since the 2004 publication of the article, "Focus on Research: Advocating for Recognition of DSI Progress in DSI Research."

The name of the foundation has been changed to the Sensory Processing Disorder (SPD) Foundation (formerly the KID Foundation). The mission remains the same: producing research, implementing education, and continuing advocacy for children with SPD and their families.

Increasing Awareness and Providing Information

An initial step toward increasing awareness and gaining recognition was clarifying terminology. Leaders in the field identified a need to update the diagnostic terminology used in sensory integration dysfunction (at that time sometimes called *dysfunction in sensory integration,* or DSI). The goal was to differentiate the disorder from the theory and the intervention, all called *sensory integration,* as well as to use a diagnostic term that is more consistent with a medical perspective. The new nosology, proposed in the final taxonomy, uses *sensory processing disorder* as an umbrella term to label the condition of individuals who have deficits in detecting, interpreting, and responding appropriately to sensory input. This term was selected because the word "process" captures the series of steps that are disrupted in individuals who have this difficulty.

In the final nosology, proposed are three primary patterns of SPD: sensory modulation disorder (SMD), sensory-based motor disorder (SBMD), and sensory discrimination disorder (SDD), with specific subtypes in each primary pattern (SMD: sensory overresponsivity, sensory

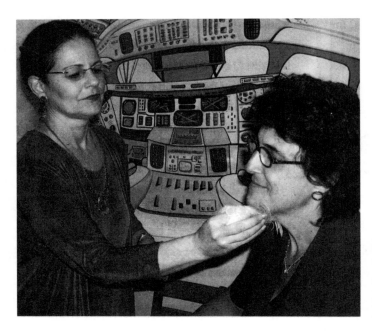

Dr. Miller (left) with Carol Margolin (right), a consultant for the KID Foundation at the Denver lab.

underresponsivity, and sensory seeking/craving; SBMD: postural disorder and dyspraxia; SDD: visual, auditory, tactile, vestibular, proprioceptive, olfactory, and gustatory). Further proposed was that the treatment will be referred to as *occupational therapy* using a sensory integration approach and the theory to be referred to as *sensory integration theory,* based on the work of Dr A. Jean Ayres.

Supporting Advocacy and Research

Since 2004, when the original article was published, the Sensory Processing Disorder Foundation has spearheaded an initiative to include SPD as a diagnosis in medical, psychological, and other published diagnostic manuals for young children. We were successful in two such efforts: DC-0-3 (Zero to Three, 2005) and the *Diagnostic Manual for Infancy and Early Childhood* (2005).

In addition, through our efforts, a research collaborative was formalized in 2004, called the Sensory Processing Disorder Scientific Work Group. This group comprises about 30 U.S. National Institutes of Health–funded researchers and faculty from some of the most prestigious institutions in the U.S. and abroad, including Harvard Medical School, Yale University, Duke University, University of Wisconsin at Madison, University of California at San Francisco, and many others. The work of the scientific work group is directed toward answering several diverse questions:

1. What is (are) the underlying physiological, neurological, and biochemical mechanisms implicated in SPD?

2. What is the evidence that SPD is a valid and separate condition from other developmental disorders?

3. What is (are) the behavioral phenotype(s) of SPD? What are necessary and specific signs and symptoms for a diagnosis of SPD?

4. Which treatments for SPD work effectively?

5. What is the prevalence of SPD in the general population and in individuals with disabilities?

6. What are the causes of SPD?

7. What is the developmental trajectory of SPD?

The culmination of the scientific work group's most recent research provided essential data that were collected and reviewed in the final application for acceptance of SPD into the 2012 publication of the *Diagnostic and Statistical Manual.* The final report was submitted to the DSM committee on August 15, 2009. We await notification of our success.

Major Evolution in Research on SPD

Since the 2004 publication for *S.I. Focus* that follows, we completed our randomized clinical trial supporting the effectiveness of occupational therapy by using a sensory integration approach for children with SPD. We received funding to initiate a collaborative occupational therapy research group, funding psychophysiology laboratories in five sites across the country that are now conducting studies by using measures of autonomic nervous system functioning (sympathetic nervous system and parasympathetic nervous system measures). Additional studies focusing on measures of the central nervous system have also been initiated and are being used to further characterize the disorder in our lab and by others by using functional magnetic resonance imaging, as well as event-related potentials. In addition, twin studies, nonhuman primate studies, pharmacology studies, epidemiological studies, family heritability studies, and more are underway.

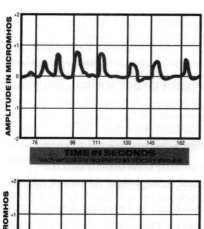

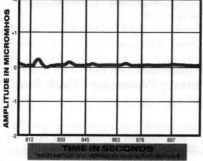

It is a promising era for children with SPD and their families. After decades of being told that "there is no such thing as sensory integration dysfunction," the empirical research data suggest quite the opposite. Times are changing, and the next time someone tells you, "There is no research about sensory integration or SPD," you can tell them, "Oh, that's so eighties!"

ORIGINAL ARTICLE

The Foundation for Knowledge In Development (KID Foundation) is a Colorado 501(c)(3) public charity, founded in 1979 by Lucy Jane Miller, PhD, OTR, to serve children with dysfunction in sensory integration (DSI). The mission of the KID Foundation is increasing awareness about the nature and severity of sensory integration dysfunction; providing information and resources to families, educators, physicians, and other healthcare professionals; and supporting advocacy for and research on DSI.

A primary vehicle for increasing awareness and providing information about DSI is the KID Foundation Web site: *www.SInetwork.org.* This Web site serves as a hub for the dissemination of information to parents, educators, physicians, and therapists. Links to current media reports on DSI, resources for books and tapes, current continuing education opportunities, and other specialized Web sites are posted. A primary goal of *SInetwork.org* is to encourage and support DSI Parent Connections, a grass-roots parent-to parent network, currently active in 32 states. Through group discussions, education, resources, and guest speakers, DSI Parent Connections provides support and information to anyone dealing with DSI. *SInetwork.org* also provides a large database of references related to DSI, frequently-asked questions by physicians and therapists, and a large number of informational fact sheets. We are beginning a new research section, with brief reviews of current research.

Although DSI has been recognized clinically since the 1960s,[1] DSI has not yet been accepted in the medical or psychological fields as a valid syndrome. A primary mission of the KID Foundation is advocating for the acceptance of DSI into the revision of the *Diagnostic and Statistical Manual of Mental Disorders,* or DSM-IV, and the revision of the Diagnostic Classification 0-3, or DC: 0-3. Recognition of DSI as a valid diagnosis will facilitate insurance coverage and referrals for therapy from physicians. To achieve this goal, research must provide convergent and discriminant empirical evidence about the diagnostic criteria that can lead to a differential diagnosis of DSI. Toward this end, Dr Miller and the KID Foundation founded the STAR (Sensory Integration Treatment And Research) Center in 1995 at The Children's Hospital of Denver, which is affiliated with the University of Colorado medical school.

With the aid of federal funding from the National Institutes of Health, as well as private funding from a variety of sources (eg, the Wallace Research Foundation, American Occupational Therapy Foundation, Coleman Institute for Developmental Disabilities, Health One, Cure Autism Now, Spiral Foundation, and The Children's Hospital Research Institute), a full-time program of research in DSI is conducted at the STAR Center. A state-of-the-art psychophysiology lab, designed as a pretend "space ship," provides sensory stimuli while specialists collect data on sympathetic and parasympathetic responses in children with DSI and other developmental disorders, in comparison to typically developing control subjects. In addition, behavioral measures provide a deeper knowledge about the functional correlates of the sensory processing disorders.

The STAR Center addresses the following research questions:

1. What are the underlying physiologic, neurologic, and biochemical mechanisms implicated in DSI?

2. What is the effectiveness of occupational therapy in ameliorating DSI, as well as in changing self-regulation, self-esteem, and social participation in children with DSI?

3. Is DSI a valid separate syndrome, or does it represent only correlated symptoms of attention-deficit/hyperactivity disorder (ADHD), autistic spectrum disorder, and Fragile X syndrome and other disorders?

4. What is the prevalence of DSI in populations with typical development and in those with various developmental disorders?

5. What is the etiology of the disorder?

6. Is there a familial component to the disorder?

Substantial strides have been made in addressing some of these research questions. For example, a standardized measure, The Short Sensory Profile, has been developed and validated for helping differentiate typically developing children from children with DSI.[2] Researchers of a prevalence estimate study conservatively estimate that 5% of children have symptoms of clinically significant DSI.[3] Data suggest that groups of individuals within the categories of Fragile X syndrome, autistic spectrum disorder, ADHD, and idiopathic sensory processing disorders all have atypical physiologic and behavioral responses to sensory processing.[4-5] Empirical evidence suggests that DSI is a valid syndrome that may be differentiated from ADHD. Finally, results of a carefully controlled pilot study suggest that occupational therapy is effective in remediating some attentional, emotional, and sensory aspects and activities of daily-living deficits in children who receive twice-weekly occupational therapy for 20 weeks. Researchers in a randomized clinical trial on the comparison of occupational therapy with a "sham" treatment, the Activity Protocol, have, to date, almost concluded their examination of the effectiveness of occupational therapy in children with DSI.

Promising pilot results indicate that children with DSI may also be differentiated from control subjects on the basis of lower heart-rate variability measures.[6] Results of these two studies suggest that children with DSI respond to sensory stimulation with increased sympathetic nervous system reactivity, as indexed by electrodermal response, and with decreased parasympathetic reactivity, as indexed by the heart-rate variability measure of vagal tone. These studies represent an important step in elucidating the underlying mechanisms in DSI.

Significant progress has certainly occurred! Clearly, much more research is needed and *must be published* to facilitate acceptance of DSI as a valid syndrome and occupational therapy as an effective treatment modality. Our program has had some initial support from the National Institutes of Health, and we are continuing to submit applications. However, funding for continuation of our research program is uncertain. The program of research is at risk of being discontinued at the medical school, due to a lack of stable and consistent funding support. With appropriate support, this research program can grow and will provide answers about DSI, as well as effectiveness data to validate the intervention efforts of therapists who so diligently care for their clients. The outcomes of our research can spawn a whole new generation of researchers focusing on the research questions outlined previously. Right now we need YOUR help to continue this research program. We are seeking individuals who have or who know clients who have access to private funding (foundations or corporate support). Individual tax-deductible contributions are also extremely important to this effort (no donation is too small to help). The field is on the brink of a revolution in knowledge about and acceptance of DSI. We are poised to finish a groundbreaking randomized clinical trial to evaluate the effectiveness of occupational therapy with children who have DSI. We are about to initiate a new generation of psychophysiologic studies with electrodermal reactivity, vagal tone, and electroencephalography measures, using automated equipment donated by PlayAway, Inc. We have initiated talks with the DSM–V committee and with the DC: 0-3 revision committee. We have obtained funding to start replication research labs at three other sites that can provide cross-validation of results. We have hosted a symposium to engage established researchers outside of occupational therapy in studying sensory processing. However, we need support, and we need it NOW. Assistance from YOU and other families, corporations, and individuals will make a HUGE difference in facilitating the forward momentum of this crucial program of research. Please think about the clients you have or others you know who would be willing to support this critical work at such a vital time, when insurance companies are eliminating reimbursement for services for developmental problems in general, and for sensory dysfunction in particular.

Together, we can make a difference.

References

1. Ayres AJ. *Sensory Integration and Learning Disorders.* Los Angeles, CA: Western Psychological Services; 1972.

2. McIntosh DN, Miller LJ, Shyu V, Dunn W. Overview of the Short Sensory Profile (SSP). In: W. Dunn, ed. *The Sensory Profile: Examiner's Manual.* San Antonio, TX: Psychological Corp; 1999:59–73.

3. Ahn RR, Miller LJ, Milberger S, McIntosh DN. Prevalence of parents' perceptions of sensory processing disorders among kindergarten children. *Am J Occup Ther.* 2004;58:287–293.

4. Miller, LJ, McIntosh DN, McGrath J, et al. Electrodermal responses to sensory stimuli in individuals with Fragile X syndrome: a preliminary report. *Am J Med Genetics.* 1999;83(4):268–279.

5. Miller LJ, Reisman JE, McIntosh DN, Simon J. An ecological model of sensory modulation: performance of children with Fragile X syndrome, autism, attention-deficit/hyperactivity disorder, and sensory modulation dysfunction. In: Roley SS, Blanche EI, Schaaf RC, eds. *Understanding the Nature of Sensory Integration with Diverse Populations.* San Antonio, TX: Therapy Skill Builders; 2001:57–88.

6. Schaaf, RC, Miller LJ, Sewell D, O'Keefe S. Children with disturbances in sensory processing: a pilot study examining the role of the parasympathetic nervous system. *Am J Occup Ther.* 2003;57(4):442–449.

Lucy Jane Miller, PhD, OTR, is founder and executive director of the SPD Foundation and STAR Center. Dr Miller is the author of nine nationally standardized assessments for children with special needs, 50 peer-reviewed articles and book chapters on SPD, and the book Sensational Kids: Hope and Help for Children with Sensory Processing Disorder.

Barbara Brett-Green, PhD, neuroscientist, is the former director of the Psychophysiology Research Program at the SPD Foundation and STAR Center.

INDEX

Note: Page numbers followed by *i* indicate an image; page numbers followed by *f* indicate a figure; page numbers followed by *t* indicate a table.

A

Auditory driving, 92
Auditory environments, 83
Auditory function difficulties, 14
Auditory processing, 16
Auditory rhythm, 91–92
Auditory sensitivities, 104
Auditory sensory disorder, 15
Auditory system, 85–86
    relationship with vestibular system, 85–86
Auditory processing pathways, 19
Autism, 24, 111
    high-functioning, 20, 150
    increasing diagnoses, 75
    and sensory spaces, 81
Autism spectrum disorders, 106–107
    visual symptoms, 127
Autistic children, studies on, 26
Autistic spectrum disorder (ASD), 35–38, 71–73,
        156, 163
Autoantibody attacks, 136
Autonomic arousal, 157
Autonomic nervous system (ANS), 104
    versus motor nerves, 61
    symptoms, 20
Avoiding activities and situations, 32
Ayres, Jean, 5, 6, 29–33, 53–57, 59–63, 65–69, 85,
        120, 160
Ayres Sensory Integration trademark, 149–152

B

Baby Einstein, 142
Background usage of auditory programs, 94–95
Bad behavior, 153–158
Balance as disordered sensory integration
        symptom, 6
Behavior, relationship to food sensitivities, 145–148
Behavioral attributes, listing, 31
Behavioral optometrists, 21, 128–130
Behavior modification techniques, 132–133
Behaviors, unexpressed and unnoticed, 32
Bihemispheric injuries, 14
Biomechanical approach for improvement, 35–38
Bipolar disorder, 147
Birth-to-Three Program, 4
Blackness, surrounding, 29–30
Blank-slate birth condition, 132
Blindness, overcoming, 49
Bonding, 68
Bone-conduction listening, 106

Booger Protocol, 99–100
Boogers, 97–101
Bottom-up processing, 155
Brain
    and brain stem, 19, 36, 66, 86
    sensory integration in, 150
    stimulating with auditory rhythm, 91–92
Brain cortex, 155
Brain-wave activity, 92

C

Cages, 49
Calming
    cards, 112–113
    effects, 93
    environments, 80–81
    sensory strategies, 23
    techniques, 66
Cards in therapeutic activities, 109–116
Caretakers, providing neurological enrichment, 50
Case examples, Sensory Stories, 26
Casein-free diets, 136
Case studies
    food sensitivities, 145–148
    gluten-free casein-free diets, 136–139
    The Listening Program, 106–107
    Rhythmic Entrainment Intervention, 92–93, 94
    Therapeutic Listening, 87–89
Celiac disease, 136–139
Center for Science in the Public Interest, 148
Central auditory processing deficit (CAPD), 14
Central nervous system (CNS), 35–36, 60, 71–72
Cerebellum, 66, 86
Cerebral allergies, 138
Challenging behavior, 153–158
Challenging events, 110
Cheese crackers, 136
Children at school, research on, 65–69
Children choosing own activities, 109–116
Child-to-teacher ratios, 75
Chimpanzees, 47–50
Chiropractic care
    education, 38
    solutions, 71–73
    therapy, 72–73
Chiropractors, 35–38, 36–37t
Classrooms, inclusive, 26
Clinical exam findings, disordered sensory
        integration, 7t, 8

Sensory overload, 66
Sensory overload reduction cards, 114
Sensory-processing deficits, 146
Sensory processing disorder (SPD), 35–38, 71–73,
    79–81, 85, 107
    mental health professionals and, 131–133
    psychologists and, 131–133
    vision in, 127–130
    visual processing problems in, 123–126
Sensory Processing Disorder Foundation, 159–164
Sensory Processing Disorder Scientific Work
    Group, 160–161
Sensory processing disorder (SPD) (term), 120*f*
    121–122, 159
Sensory rooms and spaces, 80–81
Sensory Space Design, Inc, 80–81
Sensory Stories, 23–27, 24*t*, 25*t*
Sensory strategies, teaching, 23–26
Sensory strategies in Sensory Stories, 24
Sensory systems
    with motor components, 123–126
    reliance on accuracy of, 66
Sensory teams, 128–130
Sensory View test groups, 129
Sentence formation skills, 141
Sequencing, teaching, 54
Serenity, facilitation of, 80–81
Serotonin, 154
Sesame Street, 142
Setting events, 158
Short Sensory Profile, 163
S.I. Focus magazine, ix–x
Single parents, 42
Skeletal nervous system, 61
Skill and compliance, distinguishing, 137
Skull, 36, 38
Snacks, 99
Snot, 98–101
S.N.O.T. Protocol, 97–101
Social engagement, 103–107
Socialization of difficult children, 60
Socially acceptable strategies in Sensory Stories, 25
Social rules, 97–101
Somatomotor adaptive response, 151
Sound
    as a form of sensory integration, 85–86
    processed in the brain, 84
    sensitivity to, 83
Sound Health music collection, 106

Spacesuits, 47–50
Spatial awareness, 125
Spatial Surround process, 105
Special-needs children, 31, 35, 38, 73
    consequences for parents, 41–44
Speech communication, functions of, 3–4
Speech-language pathologists (SLPs), 3–4
Speech therapy and occupational therapy, 3–4
Speed-regulation activities, 115
Spelling skills, 141
Spinal cord, 36
Spindle afferent sensory nerve cells, 7
Sport, teaching printing as, 142–143
Standardization of terminology in sensory
    integration dysfunction, 119–122
STAR (Sensory Integration Treatment And
    Research) Center, 162
Star Trek analogy, 66
State-sponsored programs, 4
SticKids, 109–116
Sticky moments, 111
Stimulants, use for hyperactivity and impulsivity, 16
Stimulating senses by using sensory spaces, 80–81
Stool tests, 136
Stories, sensory, 23–27
Strategy lists, 25
Stress
    in parents of special-needs children, 41
    from periods of change, 68
Stress reactivity, 104
Sublimation, 99
Subluxations, 36–37, 72–73
Summation (occupational-therapy principle), 57
Support groups for fathers, 43–44
Surface EMGs, 36–38, 37*f*
Survival-based neural networks, 85–86
Survival behavior, reduction to, 50
Survival messages, 154
Survival reactions and responses, 71–72, 157
Sympathetic responses, 162
Sympathetic systems, 157
Symptoms
    of childhood issues, 145
    of disordered sensory integration, 6–8

T

Tactile defensiveness, 68
Tactile input, 30
Tactile receptors, 98–99